AF675496

TRANSPORTATION ISSUES, POLICIES AND R&D

RECALLS OF AUTOMOBILES AND MEDICAL DEVICES

FEDERAL OVERSIGHT

TRANSPORTATION ISSUES, POLICIES AND R&D

Additional books in this series can be found on Nova's website under the Series tab.

Additional E-books in this series can be found on Nova's website under the E-books tab.

TRANSPORTATION ISSUES, POLICIES AND R&D

RECALLS OF AUTOMOBILES AND MEDICAL DEVICES

FEDERAL OVERSIGHT

JOHN PAULOSE
AND
ZHOU KIHARA
EDITORS

Nova Science Publishers, Inc.
New York

Copyright © 2012 by Nova Science Publishers, Inc.

All rights reserved. No part of this book may be reproduced, stored in a retrieval system or transmitted in any form or by any means: electronic, electrostatic, magnetic, tape, mechanical photocopying, recording or otherwise without the written permission of the Publisher.

For permission to use material from this book please contact us:
Telephone 631-231-7269; Fax 631-231-8175
Web Site: http://www.novapublishers.com

NOTICE TO THE READER

The Publisher has taken reasonable care in the preparation of this book, but makes no expressed or implied warranty of any kind and assumes no responsibility for any errors or omissions. No liability is assumed for incidental or consequential damages in connection with or arising out of information contained in this book. The Publisher shall not be liable for any special, consequential, or exemplary damages resulting, in whole or in part, from the readers' use of, or reliance upon, this material. Any parts of this book based on government reports are so indicated and copyright is claimed for those parts to the extent applicable to compilations of such works.

Independent verification should be sought for any data, advice or recommendations contained in this book. In addition, no responsibility is assumed by the publisher for any injury and/or damage to persons or property arising from any methods, products, instructions, ideas or otherwise contained in this publication.

This publication is designed to provide accurate and authoritative information with regard to the subject matter covered herein. It is sold with the clear understanding that the Publisher is not engaged in rendering legal or any other professional services. If legal or any other expert assistance is required, the services of a competent person should be sought. FROM A DECLARATION OF PARTICIPANTS JOINTLY ADOPTED BY A COMMITTEE OF THE AMERICAN BAR ASSOCIATION AND A COMMITTEE OF PUBLISHERS.

Additional color graphics may be available in the e-book version of this book.

Library of Congress Cataloging-in-Publication Data

Recalls of automobiles and medical devices : federal oversight / editors, John Paulose and Zhou Kihara.
p. cm.
Includes index.
ISBN 978-1-62100-122-5 (hardcover)
1. Product recall--United States. 2. Automobile industry and trade--United States. 3. Automobiles--Safety measures--Government policy--United States. 4. Medical instruments and apparatus--United States. I. Paulose, John. II. Kihara, Zhou.
HF5415.9.R43 2011
354.6'6--dc23
2011031638

Published by Nova Science Publishers, Inc. † New York

CONTENTS

PREFACE

In 2010, auto manufacturers recalled more vehicles than any other year, according to the National Highway Traffic Safety Administration (NHTSA), the federal oversight authority for vehicle recalls. However, many recalled vehicles are never fixed, posing a risk to vehicle operators, other drivers and pedestrians. Recalls are also an important tool to mitigate serious health consequences associated with defective or unsafe medical devices. Typically, a recall is voluntarily initiated by the firm that manufactured the device. This book explores the federal oversight recalls of automobiles and medical devices with a focus on developing enhanced procedures and criteria for assessing the effectiveness of recalls.

Chapter 1- In 2010, auto manufacturers recalled more vehicles than any other year, according to the National Highway Traffic Safety Administration (NHTSA), the federal oversight authority for vehicle recalls. However, many recalled vehicles are never fixed, posing a risk to vehicle operators, other drivers, and pedestrians. After the recent recalls of Toyota vehicles, Congress raised questions about the auto safety defect recall process, including the sufficiency of NHTSA's oversight authorities and whether vehicle owners are being effectively motivated to comply with recalls.

Chapter 2- Recalls are an important tool to mitigate serious health consequences associated with defective or unsafe medical devices. Typically, a recall is voluntarily initiated by the firm that manufactured the device. The Food and Drug Administration (FDA), an agency within the Department of Health and Human Services (HHS), oversees implementation of the recall. FDA classifies recalls based on health risks of using the recalled device—class I recalls present the highest risk (including death), followed by class II and class III. FDA also determines whether a firm has effectively implemented a recall, and when a recall can be terminated. This report identifies (1) the numbers and characteristics of medical device recalls and FDA's use of this information to aid its oversight, and (2) the extent to which the process ensures the effective implementation and termination of the highest-risk recalls. GAO interviewed FDA officials and examined information on medical device recalls initiated and reported from 2005 through 2009, and reviewed FDA's documentation for a sample of 53 (40 percent) of class I recalls initiated during this period.

In: Recalls of Automobiles and Medical Devices … ISBN: 978-1-62100-122-5
Editors: J. Paulose and Z. Kihara © 2012 Nova Science Publishers, Inc.

Chapter 1

AUTO SAFETY: NHTSA HAS OPTIONS TO IMPROVE THE SAFETY DEFECT RECALL PROCESS

United States Government Accountability Office

WHY GAO DID THIS STUDY

In 2010, auto manufacturers recalled more vehicles than any other year, according to the National Highway Traffic Safety Administration (NHTSA), the federal oversight authority for vehicle recalls. However, many recalled vehicles are never fixed, posing a risk to vehicle operators, other drivers, and pedestrians. After the recent recalls of Toyota vehicles, Congress raised questions about the auto safety defect recall process, including the sufficiency of NHTSA's oversight authorities and whether vehicle owners are being effectively motivated to comply with recalls.

In response, GAO reviewed laws and documents and interviewed NHTSA and stakeholders about the (1) extent of NHTSA's role in the recall process, and how its authorities compare to selected federal and foreign agencies that oversee recalls; (2) benefits and challenges of the recall process for NHTSA and manufacturers; and (3) options for improving the recall process. GAO also conducted focus groups with vehicle owners to better understand their perspectives.

What GAO Recommends

GAO recommends that NHTSA (1) modify requirements for notification letters; (2) enhance and publicize its Web site (3) better use manufacturers' data; and (4) seek legislative authority to notify potential used car buyers of recalls.

NHTSA agreed to consider GAO's recommendations.

What GAO Found

NHTSA monitors manufacturers' recall campaigns and completion rates (the number of defective vehicles that are fixed) and provides information and guidance to the public. NHTSA is responsible for reviewing the planning and implementation of recall campaigns to ensure compliance with legal requirements. To this end, the agency is responsible for reviewing, among other things, the manufacturer's description of vehicles affected by a safety defect, actions the manufacturer plans to take to remedy those vehicles through a recall, and notification letters the manufacturer plans to send to the vehicles' owners. NHTSA also monitors the effectiveness of manufacturers' recall campaigns, based in large part on the data manufacturers are required to submit on completion rates. In addition, the agency provides information and guidance to the public on recalls, primarily through its Web site. NHTSA generally has similar authorities to those of selected federal and foreign agencies GAO reviewed that oversee recalls—the Consumer Product Safety Commission, the Food and Drug Administration, the U.S. Department of Agriculture, and agencies in Canada, Germany, Japan and the United Kingdom—although some differences exist in how they can implement their authorities.

Auto industry stakeholders are generally satisfied with the recall process, but several challenges may affect recall completion rates, and thus, the number of defective vehicles that are removed from the road. Manufacturers cited NHTSA's role in the process as a key benefit, reporting clear requirements and open communication. Although franchised dealerships had some concerns related to manufacturers' communication and availability of repair parts, they were also generally satisfied with how manufacturers reimbursed them. Nevertheless, NHTSA faces challenges that may affect recall completion rates; for example, focus group participants reported that 1) they preferred notification letters with certain elements and may be more likely to comply if the letters included the VIN number and clarified the severity of the defect and 2) they were unfamiliar with NHTSA's primary means of communicating defect information to the public—its Web site. Furthermore, according to GAO's review, although recall completion rates vary considerably by certain factors, NHTSA has not consistently used the data it collects to identify which factors make some recalls more successful than others. Finally, NHTSA does not have authority to notify potential used car buyers of a defect.

Based on these challenges, NHTSA has the following and other options for improving the recall process and, more importantly, recall completion rates. First, NHTSA could modify the way manufacturers must present information in safety defect notification letters and publicize information resources, like NHTSA's Web site, so that vehicle owners are better motivated and informed. Second, NHTSA may be able to use manufacturers' data to identify what factors make some recalls more or less successful than others to better target monitoring of recall campaigns and identify best practices. Finally, expanding NHTSA's recall authorities may help identify more defective vehicles and improve recall completion rates.

ABBREVIATIONS

ACRA	American Car Rental Association
CPSC	U.S. Consumer Product Safety Commission
EU	European Union
FDA	U.S. Food and Drug Administration
MLIT	Ministry of Land, Infrastructure, Transport and Tourism (Japan)
NHTSA	National Highway Traffic Safety Administration
ODI	Office of Defects Investigation
OVSC	Office of Vehicle Safety Compliance
RSS	Really Simple Syndication
TREAD	Transportation Recall Enhancement, Accountability and Documentation
UK	United Kingdom
USDA	U.S. Department of Agriculture
VIN	vehicle identification number

June 15, 2011

The Honorable Elijah Cummings
Ranking Member
Committee on Oversight and Government Reform
House of Representatives

The Honorable Edolphus Towns
House of Representatives

From 2000 to 2009, manufacturers of motor vehicles and vehicle equipment conducted almost 6,300 recalls to address safety issues ranging from malfunctioning airbags to defective child safety seats. The vast majority of products affected by these recalls were vehicles, such as cars, sport utility vehicles, and pickup trucks. In 2010, a record 14.9 million vehicles were recalled by manufacturers, according to the National Highway Traffic Safety Administration (NHTSA), the federal agency that oversees vehicle recalls. However, owners of vehicles subject to a recall do not always get them fixed, posing a risk to owners, as well as to vehicle passengers, other drivers, and pedestrians. According to NHTSA, on average only about 70 percent of vehicles subject to a recall are fixed within the 18-month period during which manufacturers provide recall completion data to the agency. After the highly publicized recalls regarding the sudden unintended acceleration of Toyota vehicles in 2009 and 2010, Congress expressed concerns about the auto recall process, including whether NHTSA has the authorities it needs and whether vehicle owners are being effectively motivated to get their vehicles remedied.

Congress has also expressed concern about federal oversight of recall processes for other products. For example, in 2008, the Consumer Product Safety Improvement Act was enacted, which gave the Consumer Product Safety Commission (CPSC) enhanced authorities regarding safety standards and recalls.[1] Similarly, the Food and Drug Administration (FDA) Food Safety Modernization Act[2] was signed into law in January 2011 to give FDA enhanced recall authority, allowing it to mandate a manufacturer to recall an unsafe food product.[3] In addition, Congress has raised questions regarding how NHTSA's authorities to regulate motor vehicle safety compare with other countries, such as Canada and Japan.

In this context, this report addresses the following questions: (1) What is the extent of NHTSA's role in the auto safety defect recall process, and how do its authorities compare with those of other selected federal and foreign agencies with safety recall authority? (2) What are the benefits and challenges of the auto safety defect recall process for NHTSA and the manufacturers? (3) What options exist for improving NHTSA's auto safety defect recall process?

To describe the extent of NHTSA's role and authorities in the auto safety defect recall process, we reviewed applicable legislation, including the National Traffic and Motor Vehicle Safety Act, as amended, relevant federal regulations, and NHTSA's guidance on the safety defect recall process. In addition, we conducted interviews with NHTSA officials about the agency's role in the defect recall process and its recall authority. To compare NHTSA's authorities with those of other federal agencies, we reviewed legislation and interviewed officials at selected federal agencies that, similar to NHTSA, have product safety oversight responsibilities, including CPSC, FDA, and the U.S. Department of Agriculture (USDA), to determine what differences and similarities exist between the agencies' recall authorities and those of NHTSA. To compare NHTSA's authorities with selected foreign agencies with safety recall authority, we interviewed officials from agencies in four countries (Canada, Germany, Japan, and the United Kingdom) about their authorities and involvement in the auto safety recall processes of their countries. We selected these agencies based on recommendations from NHTSA and industry officials with whom we spoke and to reflect a range of safety recall processes and authorities. We also interviewed auto industry organizations in the selected countries to get their perspectives on the authorities of the selected foreign agencies, as well as officials from the European Union (EU) to understand how EU legislation may impact two countries in our review, Germany and the United Kingdom (UK).

To examine the benefits and challenges in the auto safety defect recall process, as well as potential options for improving the process, we conducted and analyzed interviews with stakeholders in the auto safety defect recall process, including NHTSA, auto manufacturers, third-party data providers, franchised and used-car dealerships, rental car companies, consumer groups, and industry organizations. In addition, to determine vehicle owners' awareness of recalls, their understanding of defect notification letters, and their willingness to comply with defect notices, we convened 10 focus groups in five cities—Chicago; Dallas; Richmond, Virginia; Salina, Kansas; and Seattle, Washington. These cities were selected to provide geographic variation and both rural and urban environments. We also analyzed NHTSA data to determine the average completion rate—that is, the number of defective vehicles that are remedied—of auto safety defect recalls from 2000 through 2008 (the last year for which a full six quarters of recall completion rate data is available) and to examine what variations exist across completion rates. See appendix I for more information about our scope and methodology.

We conducted this performance audit from June 2010 through June 2011 in accordance with generally accepted government auditing standards. Those standards require that we plan and perform the audit to obtain sufficient, appropriate evidence to provide a reasonable basis for our findings and conclusions based on our audit objectives. We believe that the evidence obtained provides a reasonable basis for our findings and conclusions based on our audit objectives.

BACKGROUND

The National Traffic and Motor Vehicle Safety Act of 1966 established safety standards for motor vehicles.[4] NHTSA was established by the Highway Safety Act of 1970 to carry out safety activities, which range from setting vehicle safety standards to working with states and local communities to reduce drunken driving.[5] In 2000, in response to the highly publicized recall of Firestone tires due to serious safety defects, Members of Congress expressed concern about NHTSA's oversight of vehicle and equipment safety. Subsequently, the Transportation Recall Enhancement, Accountability and Documentation—TREAD—Act was signed into law, which enhanced NHTSA's authority to ensure that manufacturers provide the agency with early notification of potential safety defects in motor vehicles and equipment and that manufacturers quickly take actions to remedy them.[6]

NHTSA has two primary missions in its oversight of vehicle safety:[7]

- *Oversight of auto and equipment manufacturers' compliance with safety standards established by the agency.* NHTSA's Office of Vehicle Safety Compliance (OVSC) is responsible for ensuring that new vehicles or equipment comply with Federal Motor Vehicle Safety Standards.[8] By law, manufacturers must provide certification indicating that their vehicles and equipment meet these standards, a process also known as self-certification. OVSC also tests and inspects new vehicles to ensure that they meet these standards. Auto manufacturers are also expected to periodically inspect and test vehicles throughout their production period to ensure they comply with safety standards.

- *Oversight of the identification and remedy of vehicle and equipment defects that could pose an unreasonable safety risk—safety defects.* The agency's Office of Defects Investigation (ODI) conducts investigations and identifies possible safety defects in vehicles or equipment that create an unreasonable safety risk and oversees manufacturer actions to remedy them. ODI identifies and reviews a variety of information for trends that could indicate the presence of a safety defect in a motor vehicle or piece of equipment. These information sources include consumer complaints submitted to the agency and information on fatalities, injuries, property damage claims, and consumer complaints collected by manufacturer and provided to the agency. Auto manufacturers also conduct their own investigations of potential safety defects in their motor vehicles.

As part of its mission, NHTSA is responsible for overseeing two types of recalls. Compliance recalls are initiated when vehicles or vehicle equipment is determined to be noncompliant with applicable federal vehicle safety standards, as identified by NHTSA or a manufacturer. Compliance recalls have ranged from design issues with vehicle safety belts to improper placement of warning labels for airbags. From 2000 through 2009, compliance recalls accounted for about 18 percent of vehicle recalls. Safety defect recalls, which accounted for the remaining, majority share of vehicle recalls, are initiated when a defect in a vehicle or vehicle equipment creates an unreasonable safety risk, as determined by NHTSA or a manufacturer. For example, the potential for a steering column to break and suddenly cause partial or complete loss of vehicle control could represent a safety defect and warrant a safety defect recall.

Although NHTSA also oversees compliance recalls, this report focuses on NHTSA's oversight of safety defect recalls, which as previously discussed represent the majority of recalls overseen by the agency and are initiated when a defect poses an unreasonable risk to safety. In addition, we have limited our scope to safety defect recalls that have been initiated for passenger vehicles, including cars, pickup trucks, sport utility vehicles, large passenger vans, and minivans (NHTSA also oversees recalls for other vehicles, such as motorcycles, recreational vehicles, and commercial trucks). Finally, because the U.S. Department of Transportation Office of Inspector General is examining NHTSA's activities related to the investigation of potential safety defects in motor vehicles and equipment, we did not include safety defect investigations in our review.[9]

The auto safety defect recall process for motor vehicles is a concerted effort involving five stakeholders:

- auto manufacturers—businesses that manufacturer, assemble, or import motor vehicles;
- NHTSA—the federal agency that oversees vehicle safety;
- franchised dealerships—businesses that sell or lease an auto manufacturer's new vehicles;
- third-party data providers—businesses that collect and interpret data for clients and assist manufacturers in identifying postal addresses of vehicle owners with a vehicle affected by a recall; and
- vehicle owners—purchasers or lessors of a vehicle.[10]

As depicted in figure 1, these stakeholders, in particular NHTSA and auto manufacturers, engage in a number of steps during the safety defect recall process.

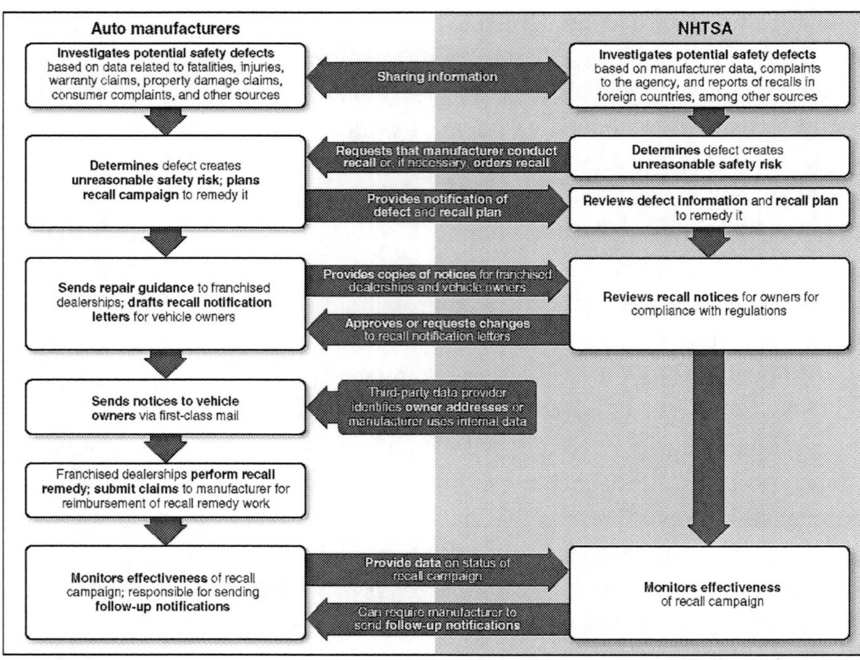

Source: GAO analysis of NHTSA documents and interviews with agency officials, auto manufacturers, and industry organizations.

Figure 1. The Role of Stakeholders in the Auto Safety Defect Recall Process.

According to NHTSA officials, since 2000 all safety defect recalls for passenger vehicles have been conducted voluntarily by manufacturers. Although some of these recalls were conducted based on NHTSA's investigations of safety defects—known as influenced recalls—most were initiated by manufacturers without influence from agency investigations—known as voluntary, or "uninfluenced," recalls (see figure 2). For example, in April 2011, a manufacturer expanded the scope of vehicles included in one of the company's safety defect recalls based, in part, on NHTSA's own investigation of the defect. Moreover, NHTSA also has the authority to order a vehicle manufacturer to conduct a recall.[11] According to NHTSA officials, the agency has not ordered any vehicle recalls since prior to 2000, and since the agency was established, it has ordered seven recalls for motor vehicles or equipment.

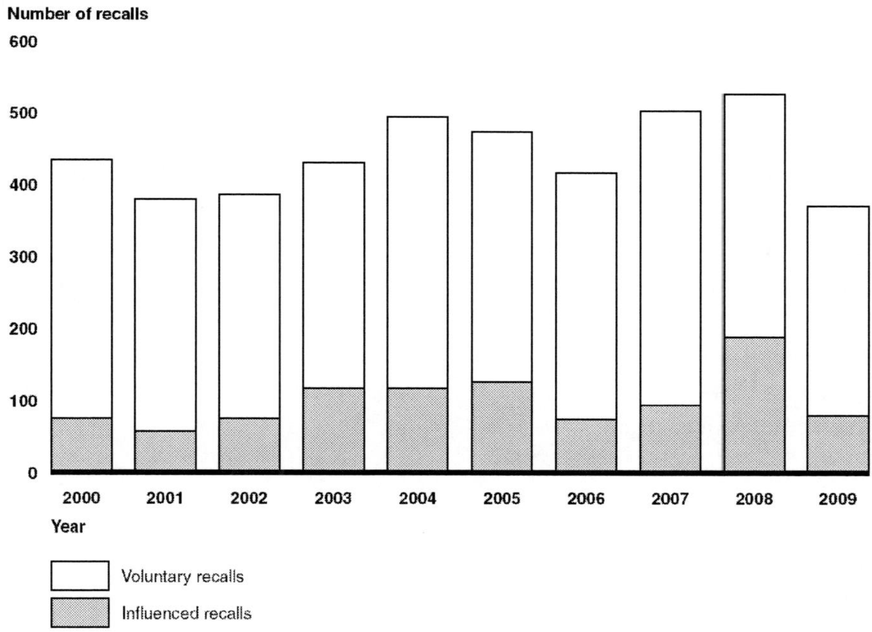

Source: GAO analysis of NHTSA data.

Note: According to NHTSA officials, the agency did not order any vehicle recalls during this time frame.

Figure 2. Total Voluntary and Influenced Safety Defect Recalls for Motor Vehicles, 2000-2009.

NHTSA Conducts Oversight of Safety Defect Recalls, and other Selected Agencies Generally Share Similar Authorities

As part of its oversight role, NHTSA is responsible for reviewing auto manufacturers' planning and implementation of safety defect recalls to ensure compliance with legal requirements. To this end, the agency is responsible for reviewing, among other things, the manufacturer's description of vehicles affected by a safety defect, actions the manufacturer plans take to remedy those vehicles through a recall, and notification letters the manufacturer plans to send to owners of affected vehicles. NHTSA also monitors the effectiveness of recall campaigns being conducted by manufacturers based, in large part, on a manufacturer's quarterly reports showing the completion rate of a campaign. In addition, the agency provides information and guidance to the public on recalls, primarily through its Web site, www.safercar.gov. NHTSA and most other selected federal agencies we reviewed generally share similar authorities in recall processes, but the agencies' authorities differ with regard to penalizing manufacturers and ordering recalls. For example, in contrast to NHTSA's recall authority over motor vehicles, FDA's recall authority over some products includes a mandatory requirement for manufacturers to recall a product regardless of any challenges a manufacturer may have to the order.[12] Foreign agencies we reviewed also generally had similar authorities to NHTSA, with a few exceptions. For example, unlike NHTSA, officials from the Federal Motor Transport Authority—Germany's agency that oversees vehicle safety—told us they can revoke the registration of vehicles with an outstanding safety recall.

NHTSA Oversees the Planning and Implementation of Safety Defect Recalls

First, NHTSA is responsible for oversight of planning efforts by auto manufacturers for safety defect recalls. Specifically, NHTSA reviews an auto manufacturer's required notification to the agency that describes a safety defect and the manufacturer's plan to remedy it through a recall.

The agency reviews several pieces of information that manufacturers must include in these notifications, including the following:

- a description of vehicles containing the safety defect, including the make, model year, and date the vehicles were manufactured;
- the number of vehicles potentially containing the defect and an estimate of what percentage actually have the defect;
- a chronology of principal events leading up to the manufacturer's decision that there is a safety defect in the vehicle; and
- a description of the manufacturer's plan to remedy the defect through a recall campaign.

As stated earlier, though all recalls since 2000 have been either voluntary recalls or influenced recalls, NHTSA can also order a manufacturer to conduct a recall. Before NHTSA can order a recall, the agency must provide the manufacturer with an opportunity to respond to NHTSA's initial decision. Prior to completion of the administrative process, the manufacturer may conduct the recall voluntarily. According to NHTSA officials, the agency tries to convince manufacturers to conduct influenced recalls based on NHTSA's investigations rather attempt to prove the case for an ordered recall through court, which the officials said can take a long time and require substantial agency resources. NHTSA officials also told us that manufacturers generally conduct a recall voluntarily if the agency informs the manufacturer that it has decided that one is necessary because, according to the officials, a manufacturer does not want to risk receiving negative publicity in an argument against the agency's decision. Similarly, some manufacturers told us that if NHTSA decides that a recall to remedy a safety defect is necessary, it is usually in a manufacturer's best interest to conduct one even if the manufacturer believes it is not necessary due to the risk of negative publicity and consumer opinion.

Second, NHTSA oversees a manufacturer's implementation of a safety defect recall. Among other things, this includes reviewing the manufacturer's letter to vehicle owners notifying them of the safety defect and the manufacturer's recall to remedy it. In particular, NHTSA reviews each manufacturer's draft recall notification letter and envelope to ensure that it includes several pieces of required information about the safety defect, meets the legal requirement to mail the initial notification via first class postage, and adequately motivates owners to make their vehicles available for remedy work.[13] Among other information, a recall notification letter must include the following items:

- an opening statement that states "This notice was sent to you in accordance with the requirements of the National Traffic and Motor Vehicle Safety Act";
- a clear description of the safety defect and the malfunction that may result from it;
- an evaluation of the risk to vehicle safety related to the defect;
- a description of what a vehicle owner can do to get the defect remedied;
- a statement of precautions, if any, a vehicle owner should take to reduce the risk that the malfunction will occur before the defect is remedied;
- a statement indicating that remedy work is free of any cost to the vehicle owners, unless the manufacturer is exempt from providing it free of cost;[14] and
- on the envelope of the notification letter, inclusion of the words "SAFETY," "RECALL," and "NOTICE" in all capital letters and in a font size that is larger than that used in the address information.

NHTSA is also responsible for receiving manufacturer notifications to franchised dealers that perform recall remedy work, which must include information about the safety defect involved in the recall, how to remedy it, and an estimate of when they can expect to be able to conduct the remedy work. According to NHTSA officials, the agency may review these notifications and provide feedback to manufacturers.

NHTSA Monitors Recall Campaign Completion Rates

NHTSA evaluates the effectiveness of safety defect recalls based on several considerations, including a recall campaign's completion rate, which, is calculated by dividing the total population of affected vehicles by the number of vehicles that have been remedied. To determine the completion rate for a recall campaign, NHTSA uses data submitted by the manufacturers. Specifically, manufacturers are required to submit completion rate data to NHTSA through reports to the agency every quarter for six consecutive quarters (18 months) after the start of a recall campaign.[15] These reports must show the total number of vehicles recalled, the number of vehicles inspected and remedied, and the number of vehicles determined by the manufacturer to be unreachable for inspection due to reasons such as theft, scrapping, or export to foreign countries. NHTSA assesses these reports against agency guidelines, or thresholds (see table 1) and considers other factors such as the severity of the defect and the amount of time since and the effectiveness of the manufacturer's last notification to vehicle owners. According to NHTSA, the agency generally uses an internal guideline on completion rates to assess whether renotification is warranted. When the completion rate is considered low, the agency may require a follow-up notification. NHTSA officials could not tell us how frequently they required follow-up notifications.

According to NHTSA officials we spoke with, after the 18-month period in which these quarterly reports are generally required, the agency can require the manufacturer to continue sending reports on the completion rate. Several manufacturers also told us that they often continue to monitor recall campaigns and send follow-up notifications beyond the first 18 months of a recall campaign whether NHTSA requires it or not.

While the factors just described provide some guidance to the agency regarding a campaign's effectiveness, agency officials told us that a variety of factors can also impact a campaign and are taken into account during the agency's review of recall campaigns. For example, agency officials told us that vehicle owners' perception of the severity of a safety defect may impact the completion rate of a campaign.

Table 1. Minimum Completion Rate for Possible NHTSA Follow-up Notification Request or Requirement

Quarter of recall campaign	Minimum completion rate (percent)
1	10
2	20
3	30
4	45
5	55
6	65

Source: GAO analysis of NHTSA document.

In addition, the officials said that factors such as the age and type of vehicles in a campaign could impact completion. NHTSA officials also told us that the completion rate of recalls with older vehicles tends to be lower because owners of older vehicles are less likely to make their vehicles available for recall remedy work. Though factors such as these can impact the completion rate of a recall campaign, agency officials told us that they do not analyze trends in completion rate data of recall campaigns.

NHTSA Provides Guidance and Information to Public

NHTSA also provides the public with guidance and information on safety recalls, primarily through its Web site, www.safercar.gov. On the Web site, NHTSA maintains a database in which the public can search for safety recalls by entering year, make, and model of a vehicle. The agency's Web site also provides basic guidance on what to do in the event of a safety recall. For example, the Web site offers guidance to vehicle owners about what to do if they do not receive a recall notification letter but believe that their vehicle may be affected by a recall. In addition, NHTSA officials told us they occasionally issue press releases and consumer advisories on safety recalls; in one case, they issued consumer advisories for a recall on faulty cruise control systems in one manufacturer's vehicles that could cause vehicles to catch fire.

NHTSA and other Federal and Foreign Agencies Share Similar Recall Authorities, but a Few Differences Exist

As table 2 shows, NHTSA and most other selected federal agencies we reviewed are generally authorized to order a recall, but differences exist in their ability to implement this authority, which we will describe in this section.

All of the agencies can impose penalties for some or all of the selected products[16]; however, there is some variation in the penalties. For example, NHTSA can currently impose fines on manufacturers up to $17.350 million for violations of requirements relating to the recall process for safety defects.[17] In 2010, the agency twice imposed the maximum penalty of $16.375 million each from Toyota for failing to timely notify the agency of defects involving accelerator pedals. CPSC can impose a similar maximum fine of $15 million, while FDA can impose maximum fines that range from $500,000 for food products to $1 million for medical devices;[18] however, the agency does not have authority to impose monetary fines for violations related to the recall process for human drugs. USDA can impose a maximum fine of $7,500 for egg products; USDA officials told us they can also impose administrative penalties.[19] For example, the officials told us that USDA can withhold the "USDA Inspected and Passed" mark of inspection, effectively shutting down a manufacturer's operations. Once a product is in commerce, USDA may detain the product and petition a U.S. court to seize it.

Table 2. Federal Agencies' Authorities to Order Recalls and Impose Penalties for Selected Products

Agency	Selected products reviewed	Can issue recall order?	Recall order is mandatory?	Can impose civil money penalties?
NHTSA	Motor vehicles	Yes	No	Yes[b]
CPSC	Consumer products	Yes	No	Yes
FDA	Foods not exclusively regulated by USDA	Yes	Yes	Yes
	Medical devices	Yes	Yes	Yes
	Human drugs	No	No	No
USDA	Meat, poultry, egg products	No[a]	N/A	Yes[c]

Source: GAO analysis of applicable laws and regulations.

[a] USDA officials told us that although they cannot order a recall, they can request manufacturers to conduct one voluntarily. In addition, agency officials told us that USDA's authority to seize and detain products was sufficient and that, therefore, authority to order a recall was not necessary.

[b] In certain cases, where NHTSA does not have authority to impose civil penalties, it can refer the matter to the U.S. Department of Justice for civil proceedings where civil penalties may be imposed.

[c] USDA can impose civil monetary penalties of up to $7,500 for egg products. Criminal penalties can be imposed for meat and poultry.

In addition, we found that while three of the four agencies have the authority to order a recall, only one—FDA—has mandatory recall authority, which sets a mandatory requirement for a manufacturer to conduct a recall based on an agency's determination of a safety defect regardless of any challenge the manufacturer may have to the recall order. Specifically, though NHTSA and CPSC have authority to order manufacturers of selected products that they regulate to conduct a recall, manufacturers can challenge either agency's order in court and during this challenge can refrain from conducting a recall campaign and continue to sell the potentially unsafe product pending the outcome of the challenge.[20] Unlike NHTSA and CPSC, FDA has mandatory recall authority, meaning manufacturers whose products are subject to this authority face a mandatory requirement to conduct a recall and refrain from distributing their product to retailers, regardless of any challenge the manufacturer may make to the order. In addition, CPSC's authority applies to retailers of products affected by a recall order, which includes a requirement for retailers to refrain from selling the affected product. Moreover, CPSC has authority to issue public health and safety findings in order to warn the public about products that the agency determines pose a safety risk.[21] CPSC officials added that in some cases this authority has proven sufficient in convincing manufacturers to conduct recalls voluntarily. FDA's mandatory recall authority applies to some, but not all, products regulated by the agency and included in our review. Specifically, although FDA has mandatory recall authority over food products and medical devices, it does not have mandatory recall authority over human drugs.

USDA is the only agency we reviewed that does not have the authority to order a manufacturer to conduct a recall, or require the manufacturer to replace or refund the cost of an unsafe product. USDA officials told us, however, that they do not consider this a challenge in addressing unsafe products regulated by the agency because the agency has the authority to detain products deemed unsafe by the agency for 20 days if a manufacturer does not do so voluntarily. FDA and CPSC also have authority to detain some of the products that they regulate.

NHTSA's authorities in the auto safety recall process are also generally similar to those of agencies with auto safety recall authority in Canada, Germany, Japan, and the UK (see table 3), with some exceptions.[22] For example, officials from all of the agencies we reviewed told us their agency can establish requirements for safety recall campaigns. Moreover, officials from all but one of the selected foreign agencies we reviewed told us manufacturers must notify them of safety defects. Similarly, officials from all but one of the foreign agencies we spoke with told us they have authority to impose penalties, such as fines, if manufacturers do not comply with laws or regulations.

However, the authorities of the foreign agencies we spoke with differed to some extent. For example, unlike NHTSA or the other foreign agencies, Germany's Federal Motor Transport Authority has the authority to revoke the registration of a vehicle for owners who have not complied with an auto safety recall notice. Specifically, the officials we spoke with from the Federal Motor Transport Authority said that if the risk of the safety defect is determined to pose a threat to persons other than the vehicle owner, then they can revoke the registration on that vehicle until the recall remedy is completed, unlike in the United States, where NHTSA has no such authority. According to the officials, in 2010, Germany revoked owners' registration due to outstanding safety recalls more than 1,000 times, and in general the agency regularly uses this authority. In addition, among the agencies we reviewed, only Transport Canada, Canada's agency that oversees auto safety, does not have the authority to order a manufacturer to conduct a recall.

Table 3. NHTSA and Selected Foreign Agencies' Auto Safety Recall Authorities

Country	**Agency**	**Requires auto manufacturers to notify agency about safety defects**	**Can order auto manufacturer to conduct arecall**	**Can establish requirements for auto manufacturer recalls**	**Can revoke registration of vehicles with an outstanding safety recall**	**Can impose penalties on Auto manufacturers**
United States	NHTSA	Yes	Yes	Yes	No	Yes
Canada	Transport Canada	Yes	No	Yes	No	Yes
Germany	Federal Motor Transport Authority	Yes	Yes	Yes	Yes	Yes
Japan	MLIT	No	Yes	Yes	No[a]	No[b]
United Kingdom	Vehicle Operator and Services Agency	Yes	Yes	Yes	No	Yes

Source: GAO analysis of U.S. laws and regulations and foreign agencies' authorities based on comments of officials representing the foreign agencies.

[a] According to MLIT officials, the agency can order users to repair their vehicles if the defects of the recalled vehicles are serious and should be removed immediately.

[b] According to MLIT officials, both criminal and administrative penalties are determined by the court according to the provisions in laws. In the case of criminal penalties, including fines and imprisonment, MLIT can report violations to the prosecutor's office. Based on MLIT's report, the prosecutors will indict auto manufacturers or employees of the companies for the violation of the law. Then based on the judgment of the court, auto manufacturers may face such penalties. In the case of administrative penalties including fines, MLIT can report the violation to the court. Then, based on the decision of the court, auto manufacturers pay fines to the government coffer.

Officials from Transport Canada we spoke with added, however, that the agency can prosecute a manufacturer on criminal charges if the manufacturer does not notify vehicle owners after identifying a safety defect. Moreover, officials from the Ministry of Land, Infrastructure, Transport and Tourism (MLIT)—Japan's agency that oversees auto safety—told us that while auto manufacturers are required to notify the agency about safety recalls, they are not required to notify it about safety defects.

AUTO INDUSTRY STAKEHOLDERS ARE GENERALLY SATISFIED WITH THE RECALL PROCESS FOR SAFETY DEFECTS, BUT SEVERAL CHALLENGES MAY AFFECT RECALL COMPLETION RATES

Although industry stakeholders were generally satisfied with the recall process for safety defects, certain challenges may affect the completion rate of recalls. For example, about half of the auto manufacturers we spoke with told us that NHTSA's regulatory requirements were clear in conveying what was expected of them in the recall process. Likewise, many manufacturers said NHTSA fostered open communication, allowing for two-way interaction that aided in prompt resolution of problems when they arose. Franchised dealerships were generally pleased with how manufacturers reimbursed them during the recall process for safety defects, although some expressed concerns, such as sometimes learning about safety defect recalls at the same time as the public and not always having the parts available for repair when recalls are announced. In addition, we found five challenges that may affect the completion rate of safety recalls:

- identifying and notifying vehicle owners of auto safety defects,
- motivating vehicle owners to comply with notification letters,
- providing better information to vehicle owners and the public,
- using existing data to improve completion rates of recall campaigns, and
- lacking the authority to require manufacturers to notify used-car dealerships of recalls and to require used-car dealerships to notify potential buyers of the existing defect.

Manufacturers Reported Clear Requirements and Open Communication as Benefits of NHTSA's Role in the Recall Process for Safety Defects

Manufacturers we spoke with were generally satisfied with the recall process for safety defects and stated that NHTSA's role in this process is a key benefit. Many manufacturers reported that the process is working well because the regulatory requirements are clear and, as a result, they know exactly what is expected of them in the process and by when. For example, some manufacturers stated that requirements for the auto safety defect recall process were well-defined and, because of this, there is little confusion about what manufacturers needed to do after a recall decision is made. Some manufacturers also reported that a benefit of the safety defect recall process is the open and cooperative communications between NHTSA and the manufacturers. For example, some manufacturers pointed out that they and NHTSA have established clear points of contact for addressing issues during recall campaigns. These channels of communication made it easier and less time consuming to resolve issues when they arose. Likewise, manufacturers told us they were generally pleased with how promptly NHTSA approved their defect notification letters—sometimes within 1 to 2 days—which facilitates their ability to implement recalls for safety defects in a timely manner.

Other benefits were cited, as well. Most manufacturers we spoke with stated that the requirement to use first-class mail to notify vehicle owners of safety defects was appropriate and effective because, for example, postal mail is a recognizable form of communication to most vehicle owners, allows uniform delivery of the same message to all affected vehicle owners, and allows the manufacturer to track the receipt of notification letters. Additionally, one manufacturer we spoke with noted that the National Traffic and Motor Vehicle Safety Act had been around for decades, and questions and concerns had already been litigated—resulting in a well-understood law.

Franchised Dealerships Reported Reimbursement for Recall Remedy Work as a Benefit of the Recall Process for Safety Defects but Expressed a Few Concerns

Franchised dealerships we spoke with generally told us they were satisfied with how manufacturers reimburse them for remedying vehicles with safety defect recalls. Moreover, several franchised dealerships told us that service work related to recalls is profitable for dealerships. One of these dealerships added that this served as an incentive to the dealer to seek out and repair used vehicles in their inventory that may have an outstanding recall.

However, the franchised dealerships we interviewed also expressed a few concerns. First, some dealerships told us that manufacturers do not notify them as promptly as they would like about recalls; as a result, they learn about some recalls at the same time as the general public through the media. Consequently, the dealership may have inquiries from customers about bringing their cars in for repair before the dealer knows about the recall. Second, dealerships expressed concern that parts are not always readily available when recalls are announced, which they said can be an inconvenience to customers who come to the dealership expecting to immediately have the remedy work completed. Two manufacturers told us that the delay in supplying dealerships with parts has, in part, resulted from many parts suppliers going bankrupt or out of business during the recent economic crisis and that they are working to address the problem.[23]

Five Key Challenges May Affect Recall Completion Rates

Identifying and Notifying Vehicle Owners of Auto Safety Defects

Some manufacturers told us that notifying vehicle owners about safety defects can be difficult for a few reasons. For example, one manufacturer said the process was challenging because not all vehicle owners keep their address information up-to-date with state motor vehicle registration offices. In addition, several other manufacturers told us that identifying the current mailing addresses for older vehicles is especially difficult because these vehicles often have multiple changes of ownership and, thus, mailing addresses, which compounds the problem. NHTSA and several manufacturers told us that the completion rates for recall campaigns with older vehicles were generally lower than the rates for campaigns with newer model vehicles, although NHTSA officials stated they have not conducted any formal analyses to confirm this. Third-party data providers that manufacturers use to collect owner information confirmed the challenges associated with identifying current vehicle owner addresses. For example, one of the third-party data providers we spoke with stated that mailing addresses for owners of newer vehicles are more current and become less reliable as vehicle ownership changes hands. In addition, they highlighted several other challenges to obtaining up-to-date information, including state privacy laws—some of which require the signature of the vehicle owner before a state motor vehicle agency can release contact information.

Focus group participants and some manufacturers we spoke with also indicated that new or additional methods of communicating recall information to consumers—in addition to the postal mail notifications currently in use—could help increase recall completion rates.[24] For example, some focus group participants indicated that they would be more likely to respond to defect notices if they received notice of the defect by phone or through e-mail, in addition to the standard first-class mailing, and some focus group participants recommended the use of multiple contact methods.

Motivating Vehicle Owners to Comply with Notification Letters

Our focus groups with vehicle owners demonstrated that NHTSA and manufacturers may face difficulties in motivating vehicle owners to comply with recall notification letters. Although manufacturers are responsible for drafting notification letters and notifying vehicle owners of a defect, NHTSA is responsible for approving the letters' contents. As stated earlier, NHTSA is responsible for ensuring that the letters contain certain items that (1) inform owners of defects in a clear and understandable manner and (2) effectively motivate owners to have their vehicles remedied. However, our focus group participants revealed that though some of them would comply with a recall notice in any circumstance, the willingness of others to comply depends on vehicle owners' perceptions of three primary factors:

- the severity of the defect—how urgent vehicle owners perceive the recall to be;
- the convenience of the defect remedy—the time projected to fix the defect, as well as whether the dealership provides an alternate mode of transportation during service; and
- the cost of the recall remedy—the perception of how much it will cost the vehicle owner to have the defect remedied (by law, a recall remedy is free of cost to vehicle owners who purchased the vehicle within 10 years of the defect being identified and, according to NHTSA, is generally provided free in all cases).

Moreover, while NHTSA has no ability to control many aspects of a recall campaign, such as the severity of the defect, the agency can control how these and other issues are presented in the defect notification letters, which may affect whether vehicle owners are motivated to comply. Focus group participants responded that they preferred letters that included certain elements. As a result, including these elements in a defect letter may positively affect whether and how quickly they respond to a recall. The focus groups we convened reviewed three defect notification letters from three separate manufacturers and indicated they would prefer the following elements in a defect letter, which may lead to higher rates of responding to a defect notice:[25]

- a clear explanation of the severity of the defect, including an explanation that does not use jargon, which can be confusing. For example, instead of using the acronym "ABS," focus group participants would prefer the words "anti-lock brake system."
- the word "urgent" to indicate the seriousness of the defect.
- a question-answer format because, as one participant described, it spells out the issue, provides an immediate answer, and allows recipients to pick and choose the parts that are most necessary to read.
- an apology from the manufacturer.
- the owner's vehicle identification number (VIN) information. As one participant explained, including a VIN in the body of the defect notification letter clarifies whether this recall applies to the owner's vehicle.
- readable font size.
- an indication of whether there is any cost involved with the recall remedy.

In addition, we asked focus group participants to review three defect notification envelopes to gauge their perceptions of the envelope style and format and the likelihood that they would be willing to open each envelope. Though the focus groups reached less consensus on what style and format of envelope they would be most likely to open, participants did reveal that they preferred envelopes that included the word "urgent," and some preferred envelopes that did not have technical or confusing language. For example, one participant stated that she liked the envelope that said "urgent air bag safety" because it described the issue in concise terms. In addition, several focus group participants liked the use of color—red shadowing, for example—to indicate the envelope's importance, and were more in favor of envelopes without VIN information on the envelope itself.

Providing Better Information to Vehicle Owners and the Public

Our focus groups revealed that many vehicle owners may not be familiar with the Web site www.safercar.gov—NHTSA's primary means of communicating defect information to the public. While the Web site is meant to provide vehicle owners and the public with valuable safety defect information, discussions with focus group participants revealed that few knew that the Web site existed or ever used the Web site to learn of recalls. For example, none of the almost 90 participants said they were familiar with www.safercar.gov and more noted that they use Google when they search for information related to safety defects.[26]

Among other things, www.safercar.gov allows vehicle owners and the public:

- to set up an RSS—Really Simple Syndication—feed that provides recall information via a computer or mobile device, updated daily, on safety-related recalls for vehicles, among other things.[27]
- to subscribe to NHTSA's Recall Notification E-mail System and elect to receive a weekly e-mail that summarizes the vehicle recalls for the past 7 days or to select up to five vehicles by make, model, and year about which to receive recall notifications.
- to search a recall database for vehicle recalls by make, model, year, and component, among other things.

However, the information NHTSA provides on its Web site could be more useful. In particular, a centralized database (developed by NHTSA or another party) that allows consumers to search for recall information by VIN would allow vehicle owners to determine if their specific vehicle is affected by a recall. Several used and franchised car dealerships we spoke with noted that having a database to search for recalls by VIN would allow those who may not have been informed of recalls through a notification letter to determine whether the vehicles they possess have outstanding safety recalls. Although NHTSA has not developed a centralized VIN database, most of the manufacturers we interviewed allow their customers to access VIN-specific recall information for their vehicles in a few ways. Some manufacturers, for example, provided their customers and the public with online access to VIN-specific recall information, but only if their customers registered on the manufacturer's Web site first. Other manufacturers, however, allowed their customers access to this information online without requiring customer registration. Seven of the manufacturers that provide online VIN-specific recall information told us it would be beneficial to have a centralized NHTSA Web page that provides links to online VIN information. Manufacturers that did not provide online access to VIN recall information allowed their customers to call the manufacturers' toll-free customer service number or sign up for e-mail notifications to obtain VIN recall information on their vehicles.

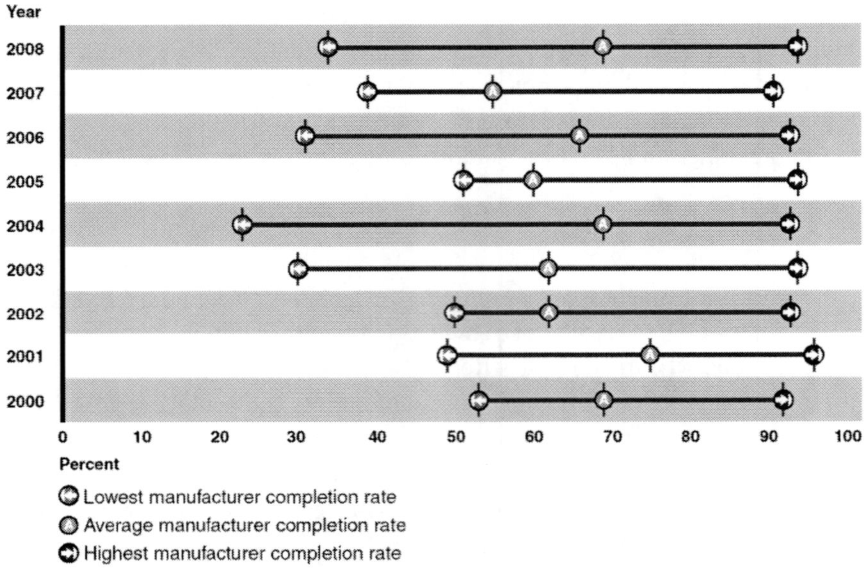

Source: GAO analysis of NHTSA data.

Note: The figure includes the automobile manufacturer completion rates for the 1,028 passenger vehicle recalls that were initiated from 2000 through 2008. The completion rate is calculated after the 6th quarter following the initiation of the recall.

Figure 3. Average Recall Completion Rates by Manufacturer, 2000 through 2008.

NHTSA officials we spoke with agreed that additional efforts could be made to improve the awareness of www.safercar.gov and told us that the agency is currently redesigning its Web site to consolidate information so that consumers can more easily find information on vehicle 5-Star Safety Ratings and auto safety recall information.[28] According to agency officials, upgrading the Web site to include VIN information would be helpful for vehicle owners but would require significant resources to implement. However, the agency is in the process of purchasing software to facilitate a VIN-based search engine on its Web site.

Using Data to Improve Completion Rates of Recall Campaigns

NHTSA is not consistently using the data it collects from manufacturers to improve the completion rates of recall campaigns. As previously discussed, according to NHTSA officials, on average about 70 percent of all vehicles subject to a recall are fixed within the 18-month period during which manufacturers provide recall completion data to the agency. However, our analysis of NHTSA's completion rate data for passenger vehicle recalls from 2000 through 2008 found considerable underlying variation in completion rates in several areas. Overall, we found that annual recall completion rates varied substantially by year—from about 55 percent to 75 percent—for all passenger vehicles with safety defect recalls, with an average across all years of about 65 percent.[29] In addition, our analysis revealed that within any given year, some manufacturers have safety defect recall completion rates as low as 23 percent to 53 percent per year, whereas other manufacturers have completion rates between 90 percent and 96 percent (see figure 3). Furthermore, some manufacturers have consistently higher or lower rates across the 9 years we included in our analysis.

Similarly, completion rates for safety defect recalls involving components—items such as brakes and fuel systems—varied from 46 percent to as high as about 80 percent (see figure 4). In particular, recall completion rates involving air bags and vehicle speed control (e.g., cruise control) systems resulted in some of the lowest completion rates across all components at 60 percent and 46 percent, respectively.

We found less variation across vehicle types; from 2000 through 2008, the average recall completion rate was 67 percent for passenger cars, 72 percent for sport utility vehicles and passenger vans, and 65 percent for pickup trucks.

Using the data that NHTSA collects to conduct a broader aggregate-level analysis across all campaigns may help NHTSA determine some of the factors that are associated with higher or lower rates of compliance. As mentioned previously, NHTSA monitors recall campaign completion rates by collecting data on a quarterly basis, including the date a vehicle owner is notified of a recall, the number of vehicles involved, the number of vehicles remedied, and the number of vehicles that are unreachable (e.g., stolen, scrapped, unable to notify owner, and so forth). In particular, NHTSA officials told us they evaluate the effectiveness of a recall campaign by comparing a specific recall campaign's progress to similar campaigns based on factors such as the age of vehicles recalled and the number of vehicles recalled. However, the agency does not currently use the data it collects to conduct a higher-level analysis across all campaigns to systematically look for potential factors related to higher or lower recall completion rates that might be helpful in identifying successful recall campaigns because conducting such analyses is resource intensive. Based on our analysis of NHTSA data, without conducting a broader aggregate-level analysis to look for outliers, patterns, or trends, the agency may be missing an opportunity to identify underlying factors that affect recall campaign completion rates.

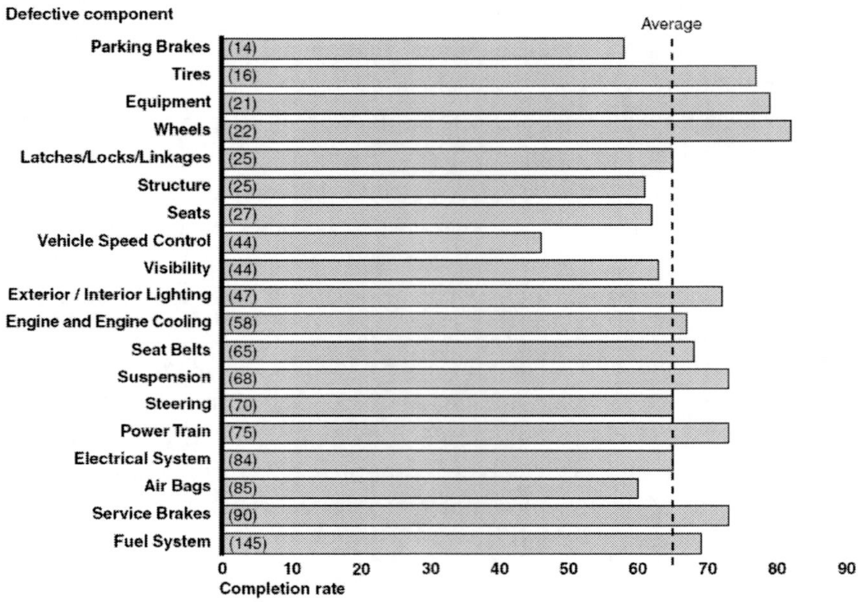

Source: GAO analysis of NHTSA data.

Notes: The figure includes recall completion rates, averaged across all years, for component categories as defined by NHTSA. The completion rates are associated with passenger vehicle recalls initiated from 2000 through 2008.

Components in the "visibility" category refer to items that affect vehicle lighting such as headlamps, side marker lamps, reflectors, and tail lamps. Components in the "equipment" category include vehicle accessories and after-market equipment, including lighting, trailer hitches, bike racks, and heated car seat covers, among other things.

Figure 4. Variation in Recall Completion Rates, by Component Recalled.

NHTSA officials told us that although their goal for each recall campaign is a 100 percent completion rate, there are a number of factors affecting completion rates that are outside of NHTSA's control—such as whether vehicle owners read recall notices or their perception of the severity of a defect. In addition, NHTSA officials explained that monitoring recalls on a campaign-by-campaign basis provides them with the flexibility necessary to capture the unique aspects of each recall campaign and that by focusing on communication and discussion with manufacturers, the agency can develop solutions to improve completion rates when a campaign is achieving a completion rate that is below its expectation. While we agree that completion rates are affected by a number of factors, including a vehicle owner's perception of defect severity, conducting additional analyses could help the agency determine some of the factors that are associated with higher or lower rates of compliance.

Limited Authorities

Under federal law, NHTSA can order a manufacturer to give notification of a defect or noncompliance with motor vehicle safety standards to the owners, purchasers, and franchised dealers, as well as order the manufacturer to remedy the defect.[30] However, NHTSA cannot require used-car dealers (or franchised dealerships that sell used vehicles) to notify potential buyers of an outstanding safety defect or require that they get the defect remedied prior to sale.[31] Used-car dealerships we spoke with told us that when they become aware of a vehicle defect, they either remedy the defect before the sale of the vehicle or notify potential buyers of the safety defect because it is a good business practice. Nevertheless, in some instances, a used-car dealer may not be aware that an outstanding safety defect exists in a vehicle. In particular, a used-vehicle dealer association with over 20,000 members told us that because used dealers do not have a franchise agreement with the manufacturers, they do not receive the defect notices that manufacturers send to franchised dealers. Moreover, used-car dealers we spoke with told us that generally they do not receive defect notices from manufacturers, except in certain cases, such as when a used dealer purchases previously leased vehicles directly from a manufacturer.

The rental car companies we spoke with each told us that, unlike used-car dealerships, they generally receive defect notification letters regarding affected vehicles in their fleets, and although they are not required to remedy a defect, they have developed a system for dealing with recalls. One company described a two-tiered system to address safety defects in which vehicles are placed on a "soft-hold"—meaning that the cars can still be rented but will be put in the queue for service—if the defect is not a safety issue. If the defect is a safety issue, these vehicles will be placed on a "hard-hold"—meaning that the cars will be taken out of service immediately and will not be rented until the repair has been made. Each of the rental car companies described a similar system that they used to address recall safety issues.

The stakeholders we interviewed had mixed views on whether used-vehicle dealerships and rental car companies should be required to notify potential buyers of outstanding safety recalls prior to sale. Several manufacturers we spoke with indicated that it was reasonable to require used-car dealerships to notify the potential buyer of a defect prior to sale. A number of the manufacturers also supported requiring dealerships to get used vehicles with safety defects remedied before selling them to the public. However, the used-vehicle dealer industry association and used-vehicle dealerships we spoke with cited a few difficulties in doing so. First, as previously discussed, used-vehicle dealers do not receive the defect notification letters that manufacturers send to franchised dealers, and as a result, they are generally not notified of a safety defect. Second, there is no single source of information on safety recalls—such as a centralized VIN database—that can be accessed to determine if a car in a dealership's possession has an outstanding recall. Instead, according to the used-car dealerships we spoke with, they must go through ad-hoc channels to find out about a defect—often by purchasing vehicle history reports such as CarFax (which may not always have up-to-date and accurate information, according to the dealerships) to determine, vehicle by vehicle, whether cars on their lots are subject to outstanding recalls.[32] Since NHTSA cannot require that used-car dealers receive notification of defects, in some cases the used-car dealers may be unable to notify potential buyers of outstanding defects. With over 35 million used cars sold by used and franchised dealerships in the United States in 2009 alone, this could pose a significant risk to the safety of millions of vehicle drivers and may have a negative impact on recall completion rates.[33]

In addition, although NHTSA has the authority to order a recall, the agency does not have "imminent hazard" authority. As initially proposed in the 111th Congress, imminent hazard authority would permit NHTSA to order manufacturers to stop further production, sale, or distribution of vehicles containing a defect found to present an imminent hazard to public safety that may result in death or serious bodily harm.[34] According to NHTSA, imminent hazard authority would allow the agency to bypass the lengthy, resource-intensive court process currently needed to prove that a safety defect exists before ordering a recall. NHTSA officials told us that if they were to obtain imminent hazard authority, they could more expeditiously enforce a recall when severe safety defects are present.

Options Exist to Improve NHTSA's Safety Defect Recall Process

Based on our interviews with industry stakeholders, our interviews with focus group participants, foreign agencies, and NHTSA, and legislation proposed in the 111th Congress, we have identified several recurring options or changes that could address some of the challenges to the safety recall process. Most of the options have both advantages and disadvantages that will require careful consideration before they are adopted.

Adopting Additional Defect Notification Methods

Notifying vehicle owners of a recall through other methods in addition to postal mail may increase recall completion rates. As we previously described, participants in the focus groups indicated that they might be more encouraged to respond to a recall notice if they were notified of a recall by methods other than postal mail. In fact, other federal agencies and some manufacturers use other notification techniques to notify consumers of a defect:

- FDA and USDA issue press releases about recalls since the owners of many products they regulate are not identifiable through a registration process. However, the level of publicity that press releases receive in the media (for example, on television and in newspapers) is subject to discretion of the media outlets, which one manufacturer noted can be inconsistent and unpredictable.
- A few manufacturers we spoke with encourage dealerships to communicate with vehicle owners through phone calls and e-mails to notify the vehicle owner of a recall and encourage them to bring the vehicle in for service.
- Finally, a few manufacturers have begun or are currently pursuing the use of telematic systems (such as GM's OnStar technology) to alert vehicle owners to recalls in real time by calling or sending messages directly to vehicles notifying owners of outstanding recalls.

However, according to some manufacturers we interviewed, there are disadvantages to using e-mail and phone calls as ways of communicating recall information to consumers. First, several manufacturers noted that vehicle owners change e-mail addresses and phone numbers frequently. In addition, they noted that there is no requirement that a vehicle owner must register a phone number or an e-mail address with a state motor vehicle agency, unlike postal mailing addresses—which are tied to vehicle registration.

Modifying Safety Defect Notification Letters

NHTSA may have opportunities to improve recall completion rates by modifying the requirements for manufacturers' safety defect notification letters. Responses from our focus group participants indicated they would prefer defect notices to include additional information, which would likely lead to higher rates of consumer responses to these notices. Specifically, as we previously noted, focus group participants reported that notification letters they reviewed did not always convey a clear description of the defect or the severity of the defect. Such confusion could affect their willingness to take their vehicles in for service and, ultimately, reduce the recall completion rates for certain recall campaigns. In addition, focus group participants indicated they may be more likely to respond to a notification letter identifying that the defect affected their vehicle specifically and that explained that vehicle owners could have their vehicles repaired at no charge.

Though some information is already required by law and regulations, NHTSA has the ability to add requirements to the defect notification letters, as previously described.[35] Rental car companies we spoke with also stated that a better indication of the severity of the recall would help them determine how to treat recalled vehicles in their fleets and reduce confusion. For example, the rental car companies told us that understanding the urgency of a safety recall is especially important because rental car companies must use the defect notification letters they receive to make decisions about whether to continue to rent vehicles to consumers before the car is repaired or ground an entire fleet of vehicles, which could result in a significant loss in revenue. NHTSA officials told us that the agency has recommended to the rental car companies that they should not rent recalled vehicles until the defect has been repaired.

In addition, NHTSA officials we spoke with told us that they review and approve each defect owner notification letter to make sure it meets the current requirements but have not developed a standard template for notification letters because each recall is different. In addition, NHTSA officials told us that although they are working toward increasing recall campaign completion rates, they believe that adding content to the notification letters could be distracting and that the fundamental information needed to convey the defect, the actions the owner should take, and the remedy program is covered by the current requirements. While we agree that adding lengthy and complex information to the notification letters is unnecessary, our focus groups have shown that a more clear description of the severity of a defect without the use of jargon and the addition of content such as the owner's VIN may encourage vehicle owners to comply with defect notifications.

Publicizing Existing Resources and Making VINs Available to Vehicle Owners and the Public

As previously described, our focus groups with vehicle owners indicated that the public may not be aware of NHTSA's Web site, the primary method of communicating information on recalls to consumers. In addition, a few industry associations told us that it would be useful to provide vehicle owners with the ability to search more easily for recall information using their VINs. As such, NHTSA has an opportunity to make vehicle owners and the public more aware of its Web site and to include more useful information. In order to so, NHTSA could develop public service announcements and additional press releases or collaborate with auto manufacturers to develop methods of informing vehicle owners about available resources. NHTSA officials we spoke with agreed that additional efforts could be made to improve the awareness of www.safercar.gov and told us that the agency is currently redesigning its Web site to consolidate information so that consumers can more easily find information on vehicle 5-Star Safety Ratings and auto safety recall information. In addition, legislation from the 111th Congress contained provisions that would have required NHTSA to improve public accessibility to information on its vehicle safety websites.[36]

NHTSA officials told us they are interested in finding additional ways to improve vehicle owners' access to specific information about recalls, and to that end, they are in the process of purchasing software to facilitate a VIN-based search engine on its Web site. However, the agency noted that developing a centralized VIN database would require significant additional resources to fully implement. In addition, agency officials told us that VIN searches can present problems because vehicle owners may not enter VIN information correctly into a Web site. NHTSA officials are currently exploring ways to address this issue.

Developing National Standards and Guidance for Vehicle Owners and Operators

Representatives of the rental car industry stated that developing guidance for vehicle owners on how to categorize the severity of a recall and whether to operate a vehicle once that determination has been made could help ensure that recalls are handled consistently and remove confusion from the process. Currently all vehicle owners, including rental companies, must decide whether to continue to operate vehicles subject to a recall based on the information provided by the manufacturer in the recall notice. The law does not require the manufacturer to advise whether the vehicle should continue to be operated until the defect or noncompliance is remedied. All of the rental car companies we spoke with, as well as some of the focus group participants we interviewed, stated that some defect notification letters are confusing and do not provide a clear description of the severity of the defect. In addition, the rental car companies noted that notification letters rarely provide guidance as to whether the vehicle can continue to be operated. Rental car company and industry representatives suggested that clear national standards—as determined by NHTSA and the manufacturers—for how to categorize the nature of a defect (including the potential for harm) and whether the vehicle can continue to be operated would be helpful to consumers and rental car companies. In particular, the American Car Rental Association (ACRA) has proposed that NHTSA issue separate bulletins for when a vehicle can be operated pending completion of a recall or when a vehicle needs to be grounded until the vehicle can be serviced. NHTSA officials stated that while they had not reviewed ACRA's proposal, they are opposed to publishing classifications of defects, ranking them, or otherwise suggesting to vehicle owners that certain safety defects are more serious than others. Moreover, NHTSA officials told us that suggesting that some defects are more risky may have dangerous consequences—namely, that many safety defects, all of which involve an unreasonable risk, will be ignored. This could result in fewer consumers remedying their vehicles due to the fact that NHTSA has categorized the recall as "less serious," and therefore, consumers may perceive the safety risk to be decreased.

Using Data More Effectively

Although NHTSA uses manufacturer data to track the average annual recall completion rate for all vehicle recall campaigns, NHTSA does not currently use its data to conduct aggregate analyses of completion rates across factors such as manufacturer, component, and vehicle type or by analyzing completion rates based on the characteristics of the defect notification letters, such as the format of the letter mailed to vehicle owners. Conducting these types of trend analyses could help NHTSA identify risk factors that might be associated with lower recall completion rates. As discussed earlier in this report, our analysis has shown that completion rates vary considerably across manufacturers and components and, to some extent, vehicle types. Additionally, NHTSA officials told us that other factors may also affect completion rates, including the perception of the severity of the defect and the age of a vehicle at the time of the recall. NHTSA has the opportunity to analyze its data in ways that capture the underlying complexities and variation in the risk factors associated with lower completion rates. With that information NHTSA could target new recall campaigns that include such risk factors and take additional steps to monitor those campaigns.

NHTSA officials told us they are interested in improving the completion rates of their recalls. For example, NHTSA officials explained that they contacted a child safety seat manufacturer that had experienced higher rates of recall completion compared with other child safety seat manufacturers, in order to learn how that manufacturer was achieving a relatively higher completion rate. While this method—isolating outliers in the data, then following up with a particular manufacturer to investigate—is not a routine monitoring activity that NHTSA performs, such an approach could be used more systematically when noticing differences in recall rates in other areas identified in the data. NHTSA officials told us they were currently re-evaluating how they used their data and would consider ways that additional data analysis could help increase recall completion rates.

Enhancing NHTSA's Recall Authorities

Legislation proposed in the 111th Congress, if enacted, would have modified the authority NHTSA has to recall vehicles. The proposed bills would have addressed some of the challenges in the recall process discussed previously in this report, such as NHTSA's authority over used-car sales and the possibility of allowing NHTSA to declare a vehicle an "imminent hazard." S. 3302 proposed a provision that would have protected potential buyers of used cars by requiring that a used-car dealer not sell or lease a used passenger vehicle until (1) the dealer clearly and conspicuously notified the purchaser or lessee, in writing, of any notifications of a defect or noncompliance that have not been remedied; and (2) the purchaser or lessee acknowledged, in writing, the receipt of such notifications. Requiring manufacturers to notify all dealerships that sell used cars about recalls and requiring such dealerships to notify potential buyers of a defect could result in increased awareness of recalls, particularly among the group of vehicle owners that, according to manufacturers and third-party vendors, are the hardest to identify through postal mail—namely second and third owners of a vehicle. However, an industry association and the used-car dealerships we spoke to noted that it is challenging to identify vehicles with outstanding recalls due to the lack of VIN data available to the public and because used-car dealerships are not required to be notified of a safety defect through the use of first-class mail. NHTSA officials agreed that notifying used-car dealers of recalls is a challenge, but the agency has not sought this authority. NHTSA officials indicated that in May 2011, however, the agency identified several policy proposals to Congress on vehicle safety issues. One of these proposals is to prohibit, with certain exceptions, used-car dealers and rental companies from selling or leasing a vehicle subject to a recall prior to the repair having been made.

S. 3302 also included a provision to enhance NHTSA's authorities to include an "imminent hazard" provision, which would have provided NHTSA with the authority to ensure that vehicles with safety defects posing a substantial likelihood of death or serious injury are recalled faster than they currently can be by giving NHTSA authority to forbid further sales of a vehicle model until the defect has been addressed. However, a number of manufacturers we interviewed stated that NHTSA's current authority is adequate; they feel the current system is generally cooperative and most passenger vehicle recalls are initiated voluntarily by manufacturers. NHTSA officials stated that imminent hazard authority would give them an additional tool to remove unsafe vehicles from the road by significantly decreasing the time and resources needed currently to order a recall through the judicial system.

CONCLUSIONS

NHTSA's oversight of the passenger vehicle recall process—one of the most important safety missions it performs—is generally considered to be balanced and effective by the auto manufacturers and other auto industry stakeholders we interviewed. However, our work has shown that NHTSA could do more to monitor the completion rates of recall campaigns and encourage vehicle owners to remedy their vehicles, which could result in removing more unsafe cars from the road. Most of these opportunities are within the scope of NHTSA's current authorities and would require minimal investment of staff and other resources. For example, our focus groups indicated that clearer communication about the severity of the defect, as well as the addition of an owner's VIN in the defect notification letter, may reduce confusion about the defect and encourage more owners to comply with the recalls. In addition, even though our analysis of NHTSA data on recall completion rates revealed considerable underlying variation in completion rates by manufacturers and defective components, NHTSA does not currently use the data it collects to conduct analyses of completion rates across recall campaigns. By doing so, the agency has an opportunity to determine the trends that may be associated with lower rates of completion and target such campaigns for additional monitoring or other actions.

NHTSA also currently lacks the authority to require manufacturers to notify used-car dealerships—which sold 11 million cars in 2009—of recalls or require these dealerships to notify potential buyers of an outstanding recall. As a result, many consumers may be unknowingly putting their lives at risk by purchasing a defective vehicle. Used-car dealerships we interviewed indicated that they may be willing to notify potential buyers of outstanding recalls; however, the lack of a public VIN database for identifying the specific cars that have been recalled makes such notifications difficult. Although additional resources may be necessary for NHTSA to implement such a database, working with manufacturers, many of whom have already developed VIN search functions, could reduce NHTSA's burden. An expansion of the information provided on NHTSA's Web site to include a VIN search capability, as well as publicizing existing and new resources, may help vehicle owners and other vehicle purveyors, such as used-car dealerships, identify outstanding recalls, improve recall completion rates, and increase safety for pedestrians and the motoring public.

Recommendations for Executive Action

In order to encourage vehicle owners to comply with safety recalls, provide vehicle owners with specific information about whether their vehicle is involved in a recall, and identify factors that affect recall completion rates, among other things, we recommend that the Secretary of Transportation direct the Administrator of NHTSA to take the following four actions:

- Modify the requirements for defect notification letters to include additional information such as (1) the word "urgent" in large type to obtain readers' attention, and (2) the VIN of the recalled vehicle so it is clear that the letter pertains to the owner's current vehicle.
- Create a VIN search function on www.safercar.gov and publicize the Web site to vehicle owners and the public.
- Develop a plan to use the data it collects on recall campaigns to analyze particular patterns or trends that may characterize successful recalls and determine whether these represent best practices that could be used in other recall campaigns.
- Seek legislative authority to ensure that potential buyers of used cars are notified of any outstanding recalls prior to sale.

Agency Comments

We provided a draft of this report to the Department of Transportation (DOT), as well as CPSC, the Department of Health and Human Services (HHS), and USDA for review and comment. DOT agreed to consider our recommendations and both DOT and USDA provided technical comments, which we have incorporated, as appropriate. CPSC and HHS did not provide comments on this report.

We are sending copies of this report to the Departments of Transportation, Agriculture, Health and Human Services, the Consumer Product Safety Commission, and other interested parties. In addition, the report is available at no charge on the GAO Web site at http://www.gao.gov.

If you or your staff have any questions about this report, please contact me at (202) 512-2834 or flemings@gao.gov. Contact points for our Offices of Congressional Relations and Public Affairs may be found on the last page of this report. GAO staff who made key contributions to this report are listed in appendix III.

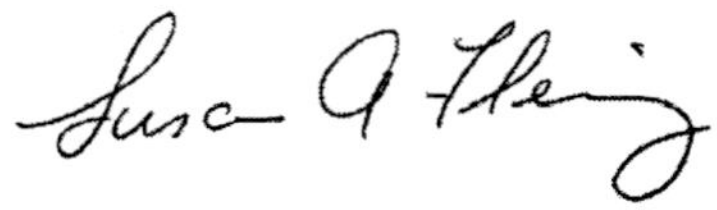

Susan A. Fleming
Director, Physical Infrastructure Issues

APPENDIX I. SCOPE AND METHODOLOGY

This report focuses on the National Highway Traffic Safety Administration's (NHTSA) oversight of safety defect recalls, which represent the majority of recalls overseen by the agency and are initiated when a defect poses an unreasonable risk to safety. In addition, we have limited our scope to safety defect recalls that have been initiated for passenger vehicles, such as cars, pickup trucks, sport utility vehicles, and minivans (NHTSA also oversees recalls for other vehicles, such as motorcycles, buses, recreational vehicles, and commercial trucks). Moreover, because the U.S. Department of Transportation Office of Inspector General is examining NHTSA's activities related to the investigation of potential safety defects in motor vehicles and equipment, we did not include safety defect investigations in our review. Our report addresses the following questions: (1) What is the extent of NHTSA's role in the auto safety defect recall process, and how do its authorities compare with those of other selected federal and foreign agencies with safety recall authority? (2) What are the benefits and challenges of the auto safety defect recall process for NHTSA and the manufacturers? (3) What options exist for improving NHTSA's auto safety defect recall process?

To describe the extent of NHTSA's role and authorities in the auto safety defect recall process, we reviewed applicable legislation, including the National Traffic and Motor Vehicle Safety Act, as amended; relevant federal regulations; and NHTSA's guidance on the safety defect recall process. In addition, we conducted interviews with NHTSA officials about the agency's role in the defect recall process and its recall authority. To compare NHTSA's authorities with those of other federal agencies, we reviewed legislation and interviewed officials at selected federal agencies that, similar to NHTSA, have product safety oversight responsibilities, including the Consumer Product Safety Commission (CPSC), U.S. Food and Drug Administration (FDA), and U.S. Department of Agriculture (USDA) to determine what differences and similarities exist between the agencies' recall authorities and those of NHTSA. We selected these agencies based on discussions with NHTSA and previous GAO reviews of federal agencies with safety recall authority.[37] To compare NHTSA's authorities with selected foreign agencies with safety recall authority, we interviewed officials from agencies in four countries (Canada, Germany, Japan, and the United Kingdom) about their authorities and involvement in the auto safety recall processes of their countries (see table 4). We selected these agencies based on recommendations from NHTSA and industry officials with whom we spoke and to reflect a range of safety recall processes and authorities. We also interviewed representatives of auto industry organizations from the selected countries to get their perspectives on the authorities of the selected foreign agencies, including the Canadian Vehicle Manufacturers' Association, the European Automobile Manufacturers Associations, the German Association of the Automotive Industry, the Society of Motor Manufacturers and Traders Limited (a United Kingdom-based auto industry organization), and the Japan Automobile Manufacturers Association. To gain a further understanding of the authorities of the agencies we reviewed in the European Union (EU)—specifically, those in Germany and the United Kingdom—we interviewed officials from the European Commission regarding the impact on member states of EU directives related to the vehicle recall process.

To examine the benefits and challenges in the auto safety defect recall process, as well as potential options for improving the process, we conducted and analyzed interviews with stakeholders in the auto safety defect recall process, including NHTSA, auto manufacturers, third-party data providers (Experian and R.L. Polk and Company), franchised and used-car dealerships, rental car companies, consumer groups (Consumers Union, Public Citizen, and the Center for Auto Safety), and industry organizations. We identified stakeholders based on our review of pertinent legislation, regulations, and NHTSA's guidance documents on the recall process for safety defects, as well as from interviews with officials and stakeholders in the recall process. We interviewed 14 auto manufacturers (see table 5) that together accounted for the majority of U.S. car and light truck sales in 2009, including those that each had greater than 10 percent market share (e.g., Ford, GM, Honda, and Toyota) and those with smaller market share (e.g., BMW, Daimler, and Hyundai).[38] We also interviewed two organizations representing auto manufacturers that operate in the United States—the Auto Alliance and the Association of Global Automakers (Global Automakers), formerly known as the Association of International Automobile Manufacturers (AIAM)—to get their perspective on the safety defect recalls.

Table 4. Foreign Agencies with Safety Recall Authority That GAO Interviewed

Foreign agency location	Foreign agency name
Canada	Transport Canada
Germany	Federal Motor Transport Authority
Japan	Ministry of Land, Infrastructure, Transport, and Tourism
United Kingdom	Vehicle Operator and Services Agency

Source: GAO.

Table 5. Auto Manufacturers GAO Interviewed

Auto Manufacturer	Manufacturers' makes included in review
BMW	BMW Mini
Chrysler	Chrysler Dodge Jeep Ram
Daimler	Maybach Mercedes Smart
Ford	Ford Lincoln
GM	Buick Cadillac Chevrolet GMC
Honda	Acura Honda
Hyundai	Hyundai
Isuzu	Isuzu
Jaguar Land Rover	Jaguar
	Land Rover

Table 5. (Continued)

Auto Manufacturer	Manufacturers' makes included in review
Nissan	Nissan
Subaru	Subaru
Toyota	Lexus Scion Toyota
VW	Audi Bentley Bugatti Lamborghini VW
Volvo	Volvo

Source: GAO.

To understand the perspective of franchised dealerships and used-car dealerships, we interviewed seven franchised dealerships and two used-car dealerships (see table 6), as well as an industry organization representing franchised dealerships, the National Automobile Dealers Association, and an industry organization representing used vehicle dealerships, the National Independent Automobile Dealers Association. The six franchised dealerships were selected to ensure coverage of multiple vehicle makes. The two used-car dealers we interviewed were selected based on recommendations from the National Independent Automobile Dealers Association.

Table 6. Franchised Dealerships and Used Dealerships GAO Interviewed

Franchised dealerships	Location
AutoNation	Fort Lauderdale, FL
Conklin Motors	Salina, KS
DARCARS Automotive Group	Rockville, MD
Fitzgerald Auto Mall	North Bethesda, MD
Honda of Seattle	Seattle
Royal Chevrolet	Richmond, VA
Sewell Automotive Companies	Dallas
Used vehicle dealerships	
Auto Buying Service	Fairfax, VA
Nelson Automotive	Mount Prospect, IL

Source: GAO.

In addition, we interviewed three rental car companies—Avis Budget Group, Incorporated, The Hertz Corporation, and Enterprise Holdings—that had nationwide operations in the United States, and an industry organization representing rental car companies, the American Car Rental Association.

To calculate recall completion rates—that is, the percentage of defective vehicles that are remedied—of safety defect recalls for passenger vehicles and to examine what variations exist across completion rates, we obtained data on vehicle recalls from NHTSA's Artemis system.[39] The Artemis system is a central repository of data on motor vehicles and motor vehicle equipment defects. NHTSA provided us with data for recalls that were initiated from January 2000 through December 2010. We limited our analysis to safety defect recalls currently being conducted. In addition, we limited our analysis to recalls initiated through 2008 because final completion rates are typically measured at 18 months, or 6 quarters, after a recall campaign begins. Including recall data from 2009 or 2010 would have biased the completion rates for those years downward; that is, they would have had lower rates of completion than earlier year recalls because the data do not extend over a full 18-month period.

Because many of the recalls conducted from 2000 through 2008 were for nonpassenger vehicles—commercial vehicles, recreational vehicles, water-craft, and trailers, among others—we eliminated all recalls that were not passenger vehicles.[40] We examined each vehicle make and model combination and coded them into three categories consisting of (1) passenger cars, (2) pickups, and (3) SUVs and vans. For example, a Chrysler 300 was coded as a passenger car, a Dodge 1500 as a pickup, and a Land Rover Discovery as an SUV. In addition, because there were hundreds of manufacturers (including those for nonpassenger vehicles) in the database—each with their own set of makes and models—we excluded all but the top 21 automobile manufacturers by market share. However, the top 21 manufacturers represent about 99 percent of all automobiles sold in the United States. Therefore, the data set we used to calculate the recall completion rates from 2000 through 2008 included a total of about 1,028 vehicle safety defect recalls after excluding nonpassenger vehicles from the database and some recall records that contained missing or anomalous data affecting nearly 125 million vehicles.

In order to make sure that our universe of passenger vehicle recalls was reasonable, we compared the number of affected vehicles associated with the 1,028 recalls we retained with the total number of affected vehicles from a report provided to us by NHTSA. Table 7 shows that, while we analyzed only about 25 percent of the recalls reported by NHTSA from 2000 through 2008, the 1,028 recalls we did analyze include 88 percent of all affected vehicles recalled for safety defects from 2000 through 2008.

To analyze completion rates for defective components by year, NHTSA provided us with a list of 387 components used by NHTSA to classify the defective component associated with each recall. We recoded these components into 19 main categories. (See table 8.). For the most part, this was a straightforward process, as the component names were grouped into similar hierarchical items such as "Suspension: Front," "Suspension: Front: Shock Absorber," "Suspension: Front: Control Arm," and so forth. All but a few of the components fit into logical, clear categories like steering, suspension, or engine and cooling. However, we had to use our judgment in a few cases, including "traction control"—which we placed in the "steering" category.

Table 7. Comparison of All NHTSA Recall Data for Safety Defects from 2000 Through 2008 to Data Analyzed by GAO

Year	NHTSA number of recalls†	NHTSA number of affected vehicles (in millions)[a]	Number of recalls analyzed by GAO[b]	Number of Affected vehicles (in millions) analyzed by GAO[b]	Percentage of NHTSA recalls analyzed by GAO	Percentage of affected vehicles analyzed by GAO
2000	432	20	163	16.6	38	83
2001	379	11.8	120	10.5	32	89
2002	385	17.6	106	15.3	28	87
2003	429	15.3	112	13.5	26	88
2004	493	28.3	151	24.7	31	87
2005	472	18.2	104	16.3	22	90
2006	415	8.7	96	8	23	92
2007	502	14.2	83	13.7	17	96
2008	527	8.6	93	6.3	18	73
Total	**4,034**	**142.7**	**1,028**	**124.9**	**25**	**88**

Source: NHTSA and GAO analysis of NHTSA data.

[a] The number or recalls and the number of affected vehicles were obtained from a report NHTSA provided us listing all recalls by year from 1966 through 2009. That report also contained information on safety defect recalls and compliance recalls. The numbers above are for safety defect recalls.

[b] These values were obtained from our analysis of safety defect recalls for noncommercial passenger vehicles obtained from NHTSA's Artemis database.

Table 8. Component Categories Used in GAO Analysis of NHTSA's Artemis Database

Parking brake	Tires	Wheels
Equipment	Structure	Latches/locks
Seat belts	Visibility	Speed control
Exterior/interior lighting	Engine and cooling	Seats
Suspension	Steering	Power train
Air bags	Electrical system	Service brakes
Fuel system	Other[a]	

Source: GAO analysis of component categories in NHTSA's Artemis database.

[a] The "Other" category was associated with only three recalls. Those recalls were not included in the component completion rate analysis presented in the report because there were so few of them.

In order to calculate the completion rate across manufacturers, vehicle types, and components, we adopted the formula used by NHTSA. That is, for each recall, we divided the number of involved vehicles reported by the manufacturer (minus those exported, stolen, scrapped, or "other") by the sum of number of vehicles corrected, the number of vehicles inspected only and not needing correction, and the number of vehicles returned to inventory.

In order to assess the reliability of the data we analyzed, we reviewed NHTSA's documentation of the Artemis system, interviewed NHTSA officials familiar with the data, and conducted electronic tests of the data, looking for missing values, outliers, or other anomalies. We did find some recall campaign records that contained missing, duplicative, or incomplete data. We had to delete 22 records from the data before we performed our analysis because there were no reported quarterly values for recall completion. Because three additional records contained duplicate reporting quarters, we deleted those duplicate quarters and were able to retain them for our analysis. We deleted a fourth recall record that had anomalous data that could not be explained. Because another recall record had an anomalous first quarter value for affected vehicles that was clearly a data entry error, we deleted that quarter's value. One final record showed a completion record of slightly more than 100 percent. We capped that record at 100 percent and retained it for our analysis. We determined by the number of affected vehicles for these questionable records that our changes and deletions have no material effect on our analysis and that the data, as analyzed and corrected, were sufficiently reliable for our purposes.

To determine vehicle owners' perspectives about safety defect recalls, we conducted 10 focus group sessions with a total of 89 vehicle owners at five locations. These sessions involved structured small-group discussions designed to gain more in-depth information about specific issues that cannot easily be obtained from another method, such as a survey or individual interviews. Consistent with typical focus group methodologies, our design included multiple groups with varying characteristics but some similarity on one or two homogeneous characteristics. Each group involved 7 to 10 participants. Our overall objective in using a focus group approach was to obtain views, insights, and feelings of vehicle owners regarding their awareness of recalls, understanding of defect notification letters, and willingness to comply with defect notices. By including vehicle owners with recent recall experience and those without recent recall experience, we intended to gather a range of perspectives regarding vehicle owners' awareness of recalls, their understanding of defect notification letters, and their willingness to comply with defect notices.

We conducted 10 separate focus group sessions—5 sessions with vehicle owners that had experienced a recall in the past 3 years and 5 sessions with vehicle owners that had not experienced a recall within the past 3 years. We selected five cities in which to conduct focus groups to provide population and geographic dispersion—Chicago; Dallas; Richmond, Virginia; Salina, Kansas; and Seattle. In addition, we used the USDA's Economic Research Service Rural-Urban Continuum Codes to select a city—Salina, Kansas—that represented a smaller, more isolated community in order to ensure we included the perspectives of vehicle owners in geographically distant or isolated communities.[41] Additionally, we used criteria in selecting participants that ensured a mix of income, gender, and educational level, and that accounted for the race and ethnicity of the area in which the focus groups were located.

Discussions were structured, guided by a moderator who used a standardized list of questions to encourage participants to share their thoughts and experiences, as well as to react to various pieces of communications. Specifically, question topics included perceived responsibility for communicating the recall, expectations for how they should be communicated with during a recall, factors that would affect their decision to bring their recalled vehicle in for service, and suggestions for improving communications of auto safety recalls. During the sessions, we assured participants of the anonymity of their responses, promising that their names would not be used. We also conducted two pretest focus groups at GAO and made some revisions to the focus group guide prior to beginning our travel for the sessions.

Each of the 10 focus groups was recorded and transcriptions were created, which served as the record for each group. Those transcripts were then evaluated using content analysis to develop our findings. The analysis was conducted in two steps. In the first step, two analysts independently developed a code book and then worked together to resolve any discrepancies. In the second step, each transcript was coded by an analyst and then those codes were verified by a second analyst. Any coding discrepancies were resolved by both analysts agreeing on what the codes should be. Because we found no differences between the recall and nonrecall groups, a document was created that compiled totals for each question, which was used for the findings that were reported.

Methodologically, focus groups are not designed to (1) demonstrate the extent of a problem or to generalize results to a larger population, (2) develop a consensus to arrive at an agreed-upon plan or make decisions about what actions to take, or (3) provide statistically representative samples or reliable quantitative estimates. Instead, they are intended to generate in-depth information about the reasons for the focus group participants' attitudes on specific topics and to offer insights into their concerns about and support for an issue. The projectability of the information produced by our focus groups is limited for several reasons. First, the information includes only the responses from the vehicle owners from the 10 selected groups. Second, while the composition of the groups was designed to ensure a range of age and education levels, the groups were not randomly sampled. Third, participants were asked questions about their experiences or expectations, and other vehicle owners not in the focus groups may have had other experiences or expectations. Because of these limitations, we did not rely entirely on focus groups, but rather used several different methods to corroborate and support our conclusions.

We conducted this performance audit from June 2010 through June 2011 in accordance with generally accepted government auditing standards. Those standards require that we plan and perform the audit to obtain sufficient, appropriate evidence to provide a reasonable basis for our findings and conclusions based on our audit objectives. We believe that the evidence obtained provides a reasonable basis for our findings and conclusions based on our audit objectives.

APPENDIX II. DEFECT NOTIFICATION LETTERS AND ENVELOPES USED IN FOCUS GROUPS

For the purposes of the focus groups, identifying information such as manufacturer names, owner addresses, and vehicle identification numbers were redacted. We distributed copies of three defect notification letters and three envelopes, as shown in the following pages:

Defect Notification Letter, Sample A (Original Included Three Pages)

(Page 1 of 3)

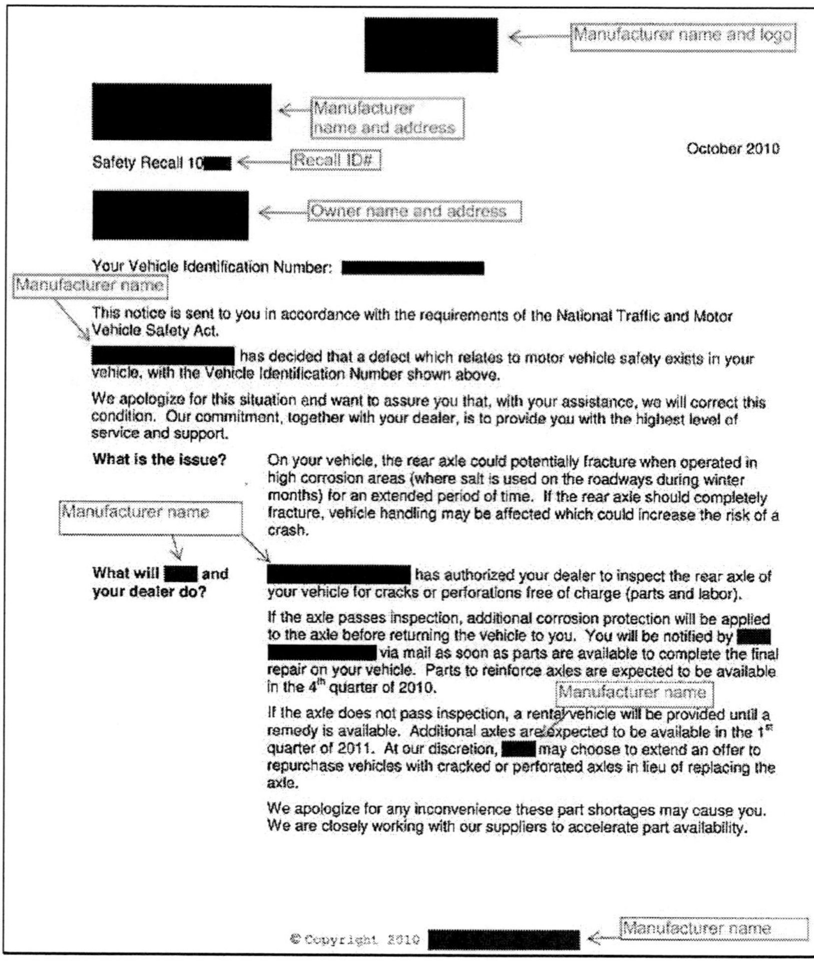

October 2010

Safety Recall 10█

Your Vehicle Identification Number: █

This notice is sent to you in accordance with the requirements of the National Traffic and Motor Vehicle Safety Act.

█ has decided that a defect which relates to motor vehicle safety exists in your vehicle, with the Vehicle Identification Number shown above.

We apologize for this situation and want to assure you that, with your assistance, we will correct this condition. Our commitment, together with your dealer, is to provide you with the highest level of service and support.

What is the issue? On your vehicle, the rear axle could potentially fracture when operated in high corrosion areas (where salt is used on the roadways during winter months) for an extended period of time. If the rear axle should completely fracture, vehicle handling may be affected which could increase the risk of a crash.

What will █ and your dealer do? █ has authorized your dealer to inspect the rear axle of your vehicle for cracks or perforations free of charge (parts and labor).

If the axle passes inspection, additional corrosion protection will be applied to the axle before returning the vehicle to you. You will be notified by █ via mail as soon as parts are available to complete the final repair on your vehicle. Parts to reinforce axles are expected to be available in the 4th quarter of 2010.

If the axle does not pass inspection, a rental vehicle will be provided until a remedy is available. Additional axles are expected to be available in the 1st quarter of 2011. At our discretion, █ may choose to extend an offer to repurchase vehicles with cracked or perforated axles in lieu of replacing the axle.

We apologize for any inconvenience these part shortages may cause you. We are closely working with our suppliers to accelerate part availability.

© Copyright 2010 █

(Page 2 of 3)

How long will it take?

The time needed to inspect the rear axle is less than one-half day. However, due to service scheduling requirements, your dealer may need your vehicle for a longer period of time.

What should you do?

Please call your dealer without delay and request a service date for Recall 10███. Provide the dealer with the Vehicle Identification Number (VIN) of your vehicle. The VIN is printed near your name at the beginning of this letter.

Manufacturer name

If you do not already have a servicing dealer, you can access www.███.com for dealer addresses, maps, and driving instructions.

███ wants you to have this safety recall completed on your vehicle. The vehicle owner is responsible for making arrangements to have the work completed. ███ can deny coverage for any vehicle damage that may result from the failure to have this recall performed on a timely basis. Therefore, please have this recall performed as soon as possible.

Please note: Federal law requires that any vehicle lessor receiving this recall notice must forward a copy of this notice to the lessee within ten days.

Do you need a rental vehicle?

If your vehicle does not pass inspection, your dealer is authorized to provide a rental vehicle for your personal transportation at no charge (except for fuel and tax) while your vehicle is at the dealership for repairs. Please see your dealer for guidelines and limitations.

Have you previously paid for this repair?

If you have previously paid for a repair that addresses the issue described in this letter, you still need to have this recall performed to ensure the correct parts and procedures were used.

You may be eligible for a refund of previously paid repairs. Refunds will only be provided for service related to a cracked or perforated rear axle. To verify eligibility and expedite reimbursement, give your paid original receipt to your dealer.

Refund requests may also be sent directly to ███. To request your refund from ███, send the refund request with all required documentation, including your original repair receipt (no photocopies), to ███.

Refund requests mailed to this address may take up to 60 days to process. Your original receipt will be returned to you.

Detailed information regarding eligibility for ███ reimbursement program and documentation requirements may be obtained by contacting the ███ Customer Relationship Center at ███.

© Copyright 2010 ███

(Page 3 of 3)

What if you no longer own this vehicle?	If you no longer own this vehicle, and have an address for the current owner, please forward this letter to the new owner. You received this notice because government regulations require that notification be sent to the last known owner of record. Our records are based primarily on state registration and title data, which indicate that you are the current owner.
Can we assist you further?	If you have difficulties getting your vehicle repaired promptly and without charge, please contact your dealership's Service Manager for assistance. RETAIL OWNERS: If you still have concerns, please contact the ████ ████████ Customer Relationship Center at ████████ and one of our representatives will be happy to assist you. For the hearing impaired call ████████ (TDD). Representatives are available Monday through Friday: 8:00AM - 5:00PM (Your Local Time). If you wish to contact us through the Internet, our address is: www.██████.com FLEET OWNERS: If you still have concerns, please contact the Fleet Customer Information Center at ████████, Option #3 and one of our representatives will be happy to assist you. Representatives are available Monday through Friday: 8:00AM - 5:00PM (Your Local Time). Or you may contact us through the Internet at www.██████.com. If you are still having difficulty getting your vehicle repaired in a reasonable time or without charge, you may write the Administrator, National Highway Traffic Safety Administration, 1200 New Jersey Ave. S.E., Washington, D.C. 20590 or call the toll free Vehicle Safety Hotline at 1-888-327-4236 (TTY: 1-800-424-9153) or go to www.safercar.gov.

Thank you for your attention to this important matter.

████ Customer Service Division

© Copyright 2010 ████████

Source: Defect notification letter used in focus groups.

Defect Notification Letter, Sample B (Original Included One Page)

Manufacturer name

SAFETY RECALL -- LOWER BALL JOINTS

Dear Owner:

This notice is sent to you in accordance with the requirements of the National Traffic and Motor Vehicle Safety Act.

has decided that a defect, which relates to motor vehicle safety, exists in some **2002 and 2003 model year vehicles.**

Manufacturer name

The problem is...	**Water may enter into the front suspension lower ball joints on your** . This can cause the ball joints to corrode and separate. Ball joint separation can result in a loss of steering control and cause a crash without prior warning.
What and your dealer will do...	**will repair your vehicle free of charge (parts and labor).** To do this, your dealer will replace the front suspension lower ball joints on all 2002 and early 2003 model year vehicles. Later 2003 model year vehicles will have the ball joints inspected and replaced if necessary. All vehicles will have ball joint boot shields installed. Shield installation and ball joint replacement (if necessary) will take about 1½ hours. However, additional time may be necessary depending on how dealer appointments are scheduled and processed.
What you must do to ensure your safety...	➤ Simply **contact your dealer** right away to schedule a service appointment. Ask the dealer to hold the parts for your vehicle or to order them before your appointment. ➤ **Bring the enclosed form with you to your dealer.** It identifies the required service to the dealer.
If you need help...	If you have questions or concerns which your dealer is unable to resolve, please contact at

Manufacturer name and phone number

If you have already experienced a ball joint failure and have paid to have it repaired, you may send your original receipts and/or other adequate proof of payment to the following address for reimbursement:

If your dealer fails or is unable to remedy this defect without charge and within a reasonable time, you may submit a written complaint to the Administrator, National Highway Traffic Safety Administration, 400 Seventh Street, S.W., Washington, DC 20590, or call the toll-free Auto Safety Hotline at 1-888-327-4236.

We're sorry for any inconvenience, but we are sincerely concerned about your safety. Thank you for your attention to this important matter.

Customer Services Field Operations

C36

Buckle up for Safety

Note to lessors receiving this recall: Federal regulation requires that you forward this recall notice to the lessee within 10 days.

Source: Defect notification letter used in focus groups.

Defect Notification Letter, Sample C (Original Included One Page in Landscape Format)[42]

SSC A0B – CERTAIN 2010 MODEL YEAR ███ VEHICLES ABS ACTUATOR ECU UPDATE SAFETY RECALL NOTICE

Dear ███ Customer:

This notice is being sent to you in accordance with the requirements of the National Traffic and Motor Vehicle Safety Act. ███ has decided that a defect, which relates to motor vehicle safety, exists in certain 2010 model year ███ vehicles.

What is the condition?

███ has received complaints of inconsistent brake feel during slow and steady application of brakes on rough or slick road surfaces when the anti-lock brake system (ABS) is activated in an effort to maintain tire traction. The system, in normal operation, engages and disengages rapidly (many times per second) as the control system senses and reacts to tire slippage. If the same brake pedal force is applied under these conditions, in the worst case, this may lead to an increase of vehicle stopping distance and thus raise the likelihood of a crash.

Each circumstance may vary, and drivers must use their best judgment, but until the remedy is completed on your vehicle, ███ advises drivers to depress the brake pedal using firm pressure. Also, please allow additional distance between your vehicle and the vehicle in front of you so as to provide additional stopping distance.

What will ███ do?

███ has developed a software update for this condition. Any authorized ███ dealer will update the ABS Electronic Control Unit ("ECU") with the newly designed software at **no charge** to the vehicle owner.

What should you do?

> ***This is an important Safety Recall***
>
> Please contact your authorized ███ dealer to install the newly designed ABS ECU software as soon as possible. The installation will take approximately 30 minutes. However, depending upon the dealer's work schedule, it may be necessary for you to make your vehicle available for a longer period of time.

We request that you present this notice to the dealer at the time of your service appointment.

If you would like to update your vehicle ownership or contact information, please go to ww███ You will need your full 17-digit Vehicle Identification Number (VIN) to input the new information.

What if you have other questions?

Your local ███ dealer will be more than happy to answer any of your questions and set up an appointment to perform this Important Safety Recall. If you require further assistance, you may contact the ███ Customer Experience Center at ███ Monday through Friday, 5:00 am to 6:00 pm, Saturday 7:00 am through 4:00 pm Pacific Time.

If you believe that the dealer or ███ has failed or is unable to remedy the defect within a reasonable time, you may submit a complaint to the Administrator, National Highway Traffic Safety Administration, 1200 New Jersey Avenue S.E., Washington, DC 20590 or call the toll free Vehicle Safety Hot Line at 1-888-327-4236 (TTY: 1-800-424-9153), or go to http://www.safercar.gov.

If you are a vehicle lessor, Federal law requires that any vehicle lessor receiving this recall notice must forward a copy of this notice to the lessee within ten days.

We have sent this notice in the interest of your continued satisfaction with our products and we sincerely regret any inconvenience this condition may have caused you.

Thank you for driving a ███

Sincerely,

███

Spanish translation on back side
Traducción en español en el reverso

Source: Defect notification letter used in focus groups.

Defect Notification Letter Envelope, Sample D

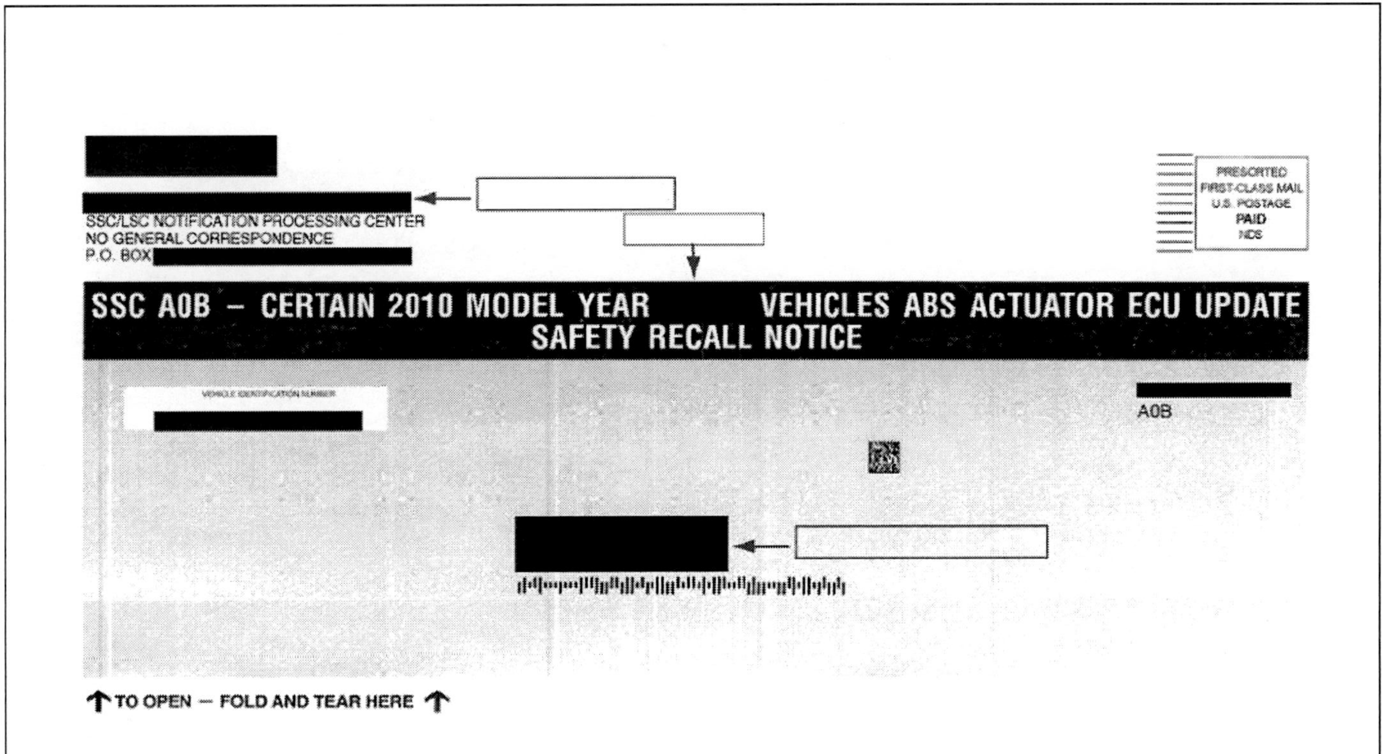

Source: Defect notification envelope used in focus groups.

Defect Notification Letter Envelope, Sample E

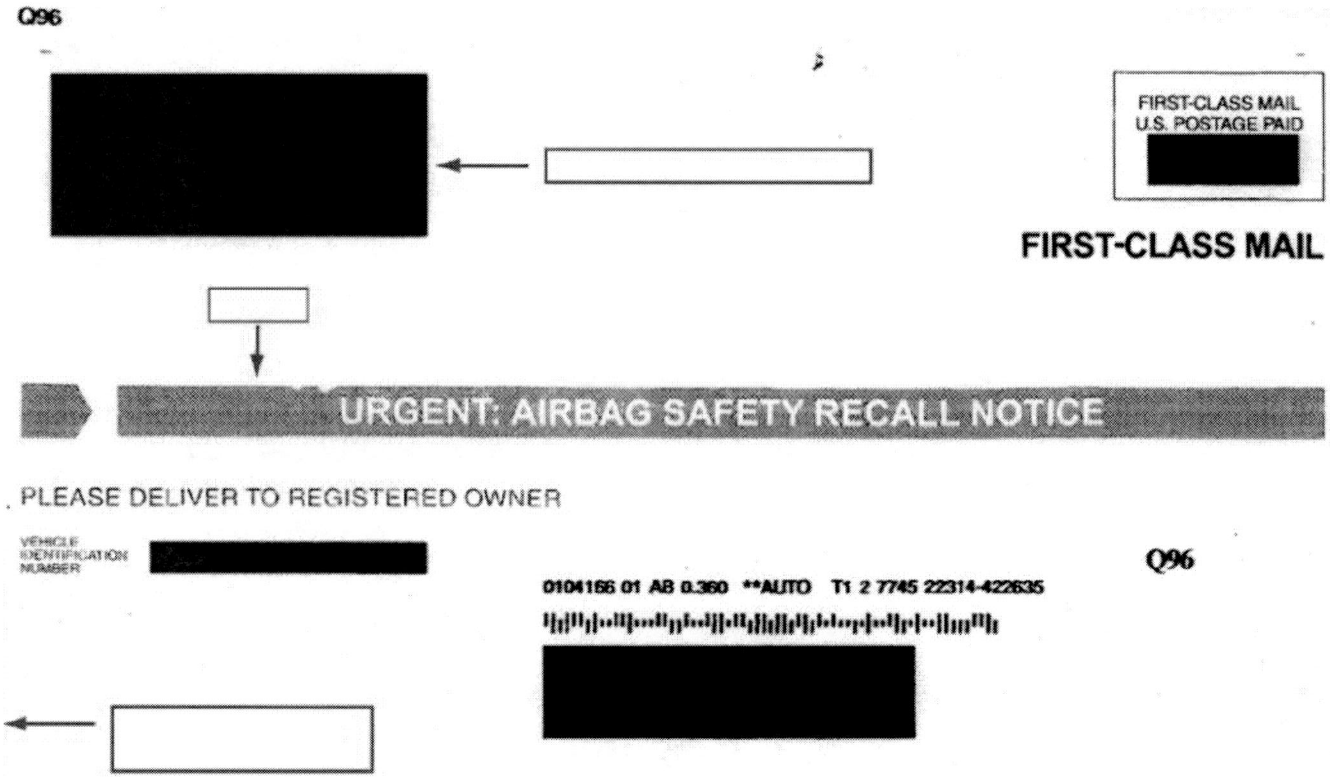

Source: Defect notification envelope used in focus groups.

Defect Notification Letter Envelope, Sample F

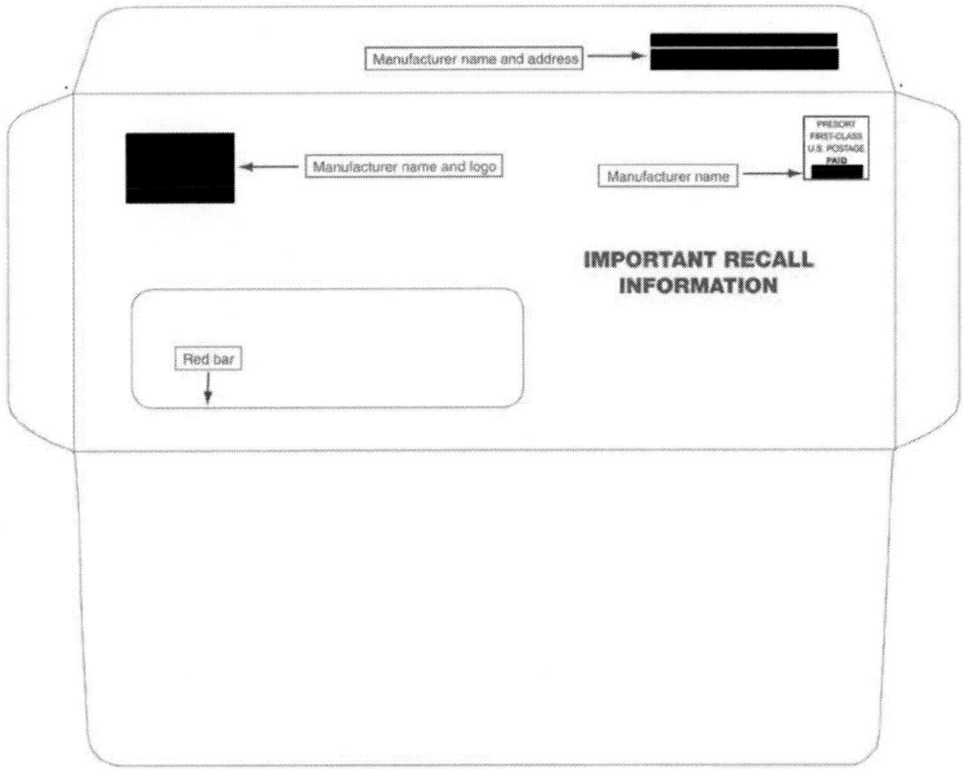

Source: Defect notification envelope used in focus groups.

APPENDIX III. GAO CONTACT AND STAFF ACKNOWLEDGMENTS

Staff Acknowledgments

In addition to the contact named above, Ray Sendejas (Assistant Director), Jennifer Clayborne, H. Brandon Haller, Terence Lam, James Leonard, Grant Mallie, Josh Ormond, Steve Rabinowitz, Amy Rosewarne, Kelly Rubin, Tina Won Sherman, Susan Michal-Smith, Andrew Stavisky, Crystal Wesco, Chad Williams, and Susan Zimmerman made key contributions to this report.

End Notes

[1] Pub. L. No.110-314, 122 Stat. 3016 (Aug. 14, 2008).

[2] Pub. L. No.111-353, 124 Stat. 3885 (Jan. 4, 2011).

[3] For the purposes of this report, a recall includes the repair, removal, replacement, or refund for a defective or unsafe product.

[4] Pub. L. No. 89-563, 80 Stat. 718 (Sept. 9, 1966).

[5] Pub. L. No. 91-605, 84 Stat 1713 (Dec. 31, 1970).

[6] Pub. L. No. 106-414, 114 Stat. 1800 (Nov. 1, 2000).

[7] NHTSA also engages in activities targeted at behavioral aspects of traffic safety—for example, through public information campaigns supporting seat belt use and against drunken driving or distracted driving.

[8] According to NHTSA, these federal safety standards are written in terms of minimum safety performance requirements for motor vehicles or items of motor vehicle equipment. These requirements are specified, according to the agency, in such a manner "that the public is protected against unreasonable risk of crashes occurring as a result of the design, construction, or performance of motor vehicles and is also protected against unreasonable risk of death or injury in the event crashes do occur."

[9] The Department of Transportation's Office of Inspector General plans to issue this report in the summer of 2011. For more information on the Office of Inspector General, see www.oig.dot.gov.

[10] Lessor means a person or entity that is the owner, as reflected on the vehicle's title, of any five or more leased vehicles, as of the date of the safety defect notification. Unless a manufacturer notifies lessees—the persons who lease motor vehicles—directly through agreement with a lessor, then the lessor is required to forward the initial follow-up notifications of a recall to lessees within 10 days of receiving them.

[11] 49 U.S.C. § 30118(b)(2).

[12] Pub. L. No. 111-353, § 206.

[13] Manufacturers are required to submit draft recall notification letters to the agency at least 5 business days prior to the date that the manufacturer plans to mail them to vehicle owners. 49 C.F.R. § 577.5(a).

[14] Manufacturers are required to provide the remedy free of cost to vehicle owners who purchased the vehicle within 10 years of the identification of the defect. 49 U.S.C. § 30120(g). However, NHTSA officials told us auto manufacturers generally provide the defect remedy work free of cost to all vehicle owners in all cases.

[15] The first quarter of reporting is required to begin with the date on which a manufacturer first sends recall notices to vehicle owners.

[16] In certain cases, where NHTSA does not have authority to impose civil penalties, it can refer the matter to the U.S. Department of Justice for civil proceedings where civil penalties can be imposed.

[17] NHTSA is authorized to impose a fine of not more than $5,000 for each violation and a maximum of $15 million for a related series of violations. 49 U.S.C. § 30165(a). At least every 4 years NHTSA reviews the amount of the fines and, if appropriate, is authorized to adjust the fines. Currently, NHTSA has adjusted the fines to not more than $6,000 for each violation and to a maximum of $17.350 million for a related series of violations.

[18] CPSC can impose a fine of not more than $100,000 for each individual violation and a maximum of $15 million for a related series of violations. 15 U.S.C. § 2069(a)(1). For food products under FDA's authority, any person who introduces into interstate commerce or delivers for introduction into interstate commerce an article of food that is adulterated or any person who does not comply with a recall order shall be subject to a civil money penalty of not more than $50,000 in the case of an individual and $250,000 in the case of any other person for such introduction or delivery, not to exceed $500,000 for all such violations adjudicated in a single proceeding. 21 U.S.C. § 333(f)(2)(A). For medical devices under FDA's authority, fines are $15,000 for each violation and a maximum of $1 million for all violations adjudicated in a single proceeding. 21 U.S.C. § 333(f)(1)(A).

[19] 21 U.S.C. § 1041.

[20] 49 U.S.C. § 30118(b)(2); 15 U.S.C. § 2064(d)(1).

[21] 15 U.S.C. §. 2055(b)(5)(d).

[22] The auto safety recall authorities of Germany and the UK are based, in part, on European Union (EU) directives. Officials from Germany and the UK told us that their national laws pertaining to the recall process are based on laws that apply to safety standards for all consumer products, which, in turn, are based on the EU's law pertaining to general product safety. EU officials told us that the EU requires that all of its member states conduct risk assessments of potential safety defects in products, such as motor vehicles, and ensure that manufacturers take actions to remedy these risks. According to the officials, member states must also report safety defects to the EU so that they can be posted to a Web-based system accessible to the public.

[23] In November 2009, a survey by the Original Equipment Suppliers Association—a leading auto supply industry group—reported that at least 43 U.S.-based auto suppliers had filed for Chapter 11 bankruptcy protection in 2009. Also in 2009, a consultant group estimated that as many as 30 percent of North American suppliers were at high risk of failure.

[24] We convened 10 focus groups of vehicle owners in five cities—Chicago; Dallas; Richmond, Virginia; Salina, Kansas; and Seattle—to determine vehicle owners' awareness of auto safety recalls, their willingness to comply with defect notification letters, and potential options for improving safety defect notification letters. For more information, see appendix I.

[25] See appendix II for copies of the three defect notification letters and three envelopes reviewed by the focus group participants.

[26] CPSC sponsors www.recalls.gov, which provides information on, among other things, consumer product recalls and auto safety recalls. Six federal regulatory agencies, including NHTSA, participate in recalls.gov. In addition to searching for safety recalls, consumers may access a list of recent recalls issued by each of the six agencies. Consumers may also subscribe to e-mail alerts from four of the six agencies, including NHTSA.

[27] Each new recall will remain available on the RSS feed for 7 days.

[28] NHTSA's 5-Star Safety Ratings measure the crash worthiness and rollover safety of vehicles. Five stars indicate the highest rating, one star indicates the lowest.

[29] NHTSA does not have a separate category in their data for "passenger vehicles." For our analysis we excluded motorcycles, commercial vehicles, trailers, recreational vehicles, and

car seats. Furthermore, we included only safety defect recalls for vehicles from the top 21 manufacturers in terms of U.S. market share according to Ward's Automotive Group from 2000 through 2008. All data for 2009 or 2010 was excluded because recall completion data for recalls initiated during late 2009 or 2010 would not have matured a full 18 months (6 quarters) at the time of our analysis. After these exclusions, our analysis included 1,028 safety defect recall campaigns representing about 88 percent of all affected vehicles recalled by manufacturers from 2000 through 2008.

[30] 49 U.S.C. § 30118(b)(2). While NHTSA can order the manufacturer to remedy the defect, according to NHTSA officials, the process of remedying vehicles is overseen by the manufacturer with minimal involvement from NHTSA. The process of remedying defects primarily involves the manufacturer and franchised dealers.

[31] Franchised dealers that sell new motor vehicles may sell or lease the motor vehicle only if the defect has been remedied before delivery of the motor vehicle under the sale or lease. 49 U.S.C. § 30120.

[32] CarFax reports are available on all used cars and light trucks model year 1981 or later using the unique 17-character VIN. These reports check for information on a vehicle's history such as title information; accident indicators, including air bag deployment; and recall information.

[33] *National Independent Automobile Dealers Association, Used Car Industry Report* (2010).

[34] Motor Vehicle Safety Act of 2010, S. 3302, 111th Cong. (2010). This bill was not enacted in the 111th Congress.

[35] NHTSA requires defect notification letters to have (1) a notation on the envelope that include the words "SAFETY," "RECALL," and "NOTICE" in all capital letters and in a font different from the address information; (2) a clear description of the defect; (3) an evaluation of the risk to vehicle safety related to the defect; and (4) a statement of measures to be taken to remedy the defect. 49 C.F.R. § 577.5.

[36] S. 3302; Motor Vehicle Safety Act of 2010, H.R.5381, 111th Cong. (2010).

[37] GAO, *Food Safety: USDA and FDA Need to Better Ensure Prompt and Complete Recalls of Potentially Unsafe Food*, GAO-05-51 (Washington, D.C.: Oct. 6, 2004); and *Consumer Safety: Better Information and Planning Would Strengthen CPSC's Oversight of Imported Products*, GAO-09-803 (Washington, D.C.: Aug. 14, 2009).

[38] Congressional Research Service, "The U.S. Motor Vehicle Industry: Confronting a New Dynamic in the Global Economy," R41154 (Mar. 26, 2010).

[39] NHTSA officials told us that they do not have a definition of passenger vehicles. Therefore, we defined passenger vehicles as noncommercial cars, sport utility vehicles, large vans, minivans, and pickup trucks.

[40] We also excluded motorcycles from our analyses.

[41] See USDA Economic Research Service at http://www.ers.usda.gov/Briefing/Rurality/RuralUrbCon/.

[42] This defect notification letter was two-sided, with one side in English and the other in Spanish. The Spanish letter (not shown) was not discussed in our focus groups.

In: Recalls of Automobiles and Medical Devices … ISBN: 978-1-62100-122-5
Editors: J. Paulose and Z. Kihara © 2012 Nova Science Publishers, Inc.

Chapter 2

MEDICAL DEVICES: FDA SHOULD ENHANCE ITS OVERSIGHT OF RECALLS

United States Government Accountability Office

WHY GAO DID THIS STUDY

Recalls are an important tool to mitigate serious health consequences associated with defective or unsafe medical devices. Typically, a recall is voluntarily initiated by the firm that manufactured the device. The Food and Drug Administration (FDA), an agency within the Department of Health and Human Services (HHS), oversees implementation of the recall. FDA classifies recalls based on health risks of using the recalled device—class I recalls present the highest risk (including death), followed by class II and class III. FDA also determines whether a firm has effectively implemented a recall, and when a recall can be terminated. This report identifies (1) the numbers and characteristics of medical device recalls and FDA's use of this information to aid its oversight, and (2) the extent to which the process ensures the effective implementation and termination of the highest-risk recalls. GAO interviewed FDA officials and examined information on medical device recalls initiated and reported from 2005 through 2009, and reviewed FDA's documentation for a sample of 53 (40 percent) of class I recalls initiated during this period.

WHAT GAO RECOMMENDS

To aid its oversight of the medical device recall process, FDA should routinely assess information on device recalls, develop enhanced procedures and criteria for assessing the effectiveness of recalls, and document the agency's basis for terminating individual recalls. HHS agreed with GAO's recommendations.

WHAT GAO FOUND

From 2005 through 2009, firms initiated 3,510 medical device recalls, an average of just over 700 per year. FDA classified the vast majority—nearly 83 percent—as class II, meaning use of these recalled devices carried a moderate health risk, or that the probability of serious adverse health consequences was remote. Just over 40 percent of the recalls involved cardiovascular, radiological, or orthopedic devices. FDA has used recall data to monitor individual recalls and target firms for inspections. However, it has not routinely analyzed recall data to determine whether there are systemic problems underlying trends in device recalls. Thus, FDA is missing an opportunity to use recall data to proactively identify and address the risks presented by unsafe devices.

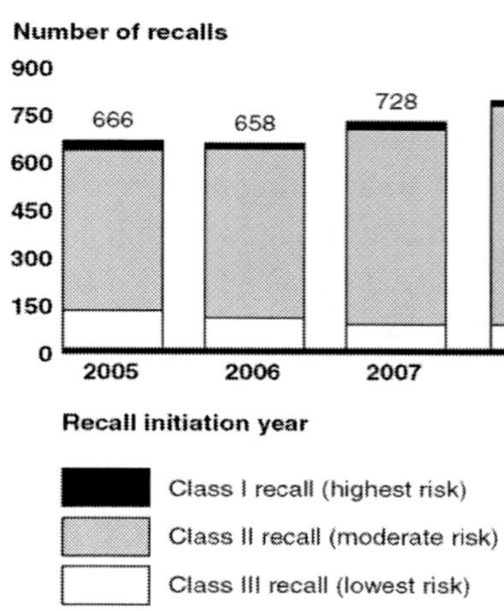

Source: GAO analysis of FDA data.

Number of Medical Device Recalls Initiated from 2005 through 2009.

Several gaps in the medical device recall process limited firms' and FDA's abilities to ensure that the highest-risk recalls were implemented in an effective and timely manner. For many high-risk recalls, firms faced challenges, such as locating specific devices or device users, and thus could not correct or remove all devices. FDA's procedures for overseeing recalls are unclear. As a result, FDA officials examining similar situations sometimes reached opposite conclusions on whether recalls were effective. FDA had also not established criteria, based on the nature or type of devices, for assessing whether firms corrected or removed a sufficient number of recalled devices. Additionally, FDA's decisions to terminate completed recalls—that is, assess whether firms had taken sufficient actions to prevent a recurrence of the problems that led to the recalls—were frequently not made within its prescribed time frames. Finally, FDA did not document its justification for terminating recalls. If unaddressed by FDA, the combined effect of these gaps may increase the risk that unsafe medical devices could remain on the market.

ABBREVIATIONS

CDRH	Center for Devices and Radiological Health
FDA	Food and Drug Administration
FDAAA	Food and Drug Administration Amendments Act of 2007
HHS	Department of Health and Human Services
ORA	Office of Regulatory Affairs
PMA	premarket approval
RES	Recall Enterprise System
UDI	unique device identification

June 14, 2011

The Honorable Charles E. Grassley
Ranking Member
Committee on the Judiciary
United States Senate

The Honorable Herb Kohl
Chairman
Special Committee on Aging
United States Senate

Each day, millions of individual medical devices produced by thousands of manufacturing establishments in the United States and overseas are used in hospitals, physicians' offices, and other health care settings to diagnose, treat, or prevent illness. For example, in 2007 medical devices were involved in 45 million inpatient procedures. Also, there were approximately 117 million visits to hospital emergency departments, 89 million hospital outpatient visits, and 994 million visits to physicians' offices, which likely all involved the use of one or more medical devices. Medical devices include those that present little risk—such as tongue depressors and elastic bandages—and those that are used specifically to sustain or support life—such as pacemakers and artificial heart valves. Medical devices are an integral part of patient care. If one proves to be defective or unsafe once it is in widespread use, the ramifications can be severe, potentially resulting in permanent injuries or deaths to patients or providers using the device.

A recall is an important remedial action that can mitigate the risk of serious health consequences associated with a defective or unsafe medical device. Generally, the firm that manufactured the device voluntarily initiates a recall after it has discovered a problem based on its assessment of complaints or reports of safety issues it has received. The Food and Drug Administration (FDA), an agency within the Department of Health and Human Services (HHS), is responsible for ensuring that medical products sold in the United States are safe and effective. In some cases, FDA identifies a problem with a device based on its own oversight, such as an inspection of an establishment where a device is manufactured. In response, the firm may voluntarily initiate a recall. Additionally, FDA has the authority to require that the firm initiate a device recall when there is a serious risk to public health and the firm has not done so.[1]

FDA's role in the voluntary recall process is generally to oversee a firm's management of a recall, which includes monitoring the progress of the recall. FDA has issued guidance to aid firms in conducting such recalls and has also established internal procedures to govern its oversight of the recall process.[2] In addition, FDA assigns each recall a classification level—high, moderate, or low—based on its assessment of the degree of risk that is posed by the continued use of the device. An effective and timely recall depends on actions taken by the firm manufacturing the device, companies distributing the device, users of the device—such as hospitals, physicians, and patients—and FDA. Recalling firms are responsible for alerting FDA, their distributors, and users of the device about the recall. The recalling firm provides instructions on steps to be taken to fix the device or advises parties to discontinue its use. These parties must follow the firm's instructions in order to effectively implement the recall.

Despite efforts by recalling firms, FDA, and others, there have been reported incidents where individuals were seriously injured or died due to continued use of defective devices that had been recalled. You expressed concern with the effectiveness of the medical device recall process and asked us to follow up on our 1998 report on FDA's oversight of medical device recalls.[3] Our preliminary findings were included in an April 2011 hearing on the reform of the medical device approval process before the Senate Special Committee on Aging.[4] This report identifies (1) the numbers and characteristics of medical device recalls initiated from January 1, 2005, through December 31, 2009, and the extent to which FDA uses this information to aid in its oversight of recalls, and (2) the extent to which the medical device recall process ensures the effective implementation and termination of those classified as high-risk recalls.

To identify the numbers and characteristics of voluntary medical device recalls, we obtained information on all such recalls initiated and reported to FDA from January 1, 2005, through December 31, 2009.[5] This information consisted of the most recent 5-year period of available data at the time we did our work. The source of this information was FDA's Recall Enterprise System (RES), the agency's central repository of recall information. FDA provided key information on each recall, including FDA's unique recall event number;[6] the status of the recall at the time FDA provided us with this information (e.g., ongoing or terminated);[7] the reason for the recall; the specific device being recalled; the recall classification level assigned based on FDA's assessment of risk; dates the recalls were initiated, classified, and terminated; and the medical specialty—area of use—for each device subject to recall (e.g cardiovascular or orthopedic). We also obtained information identifying whic of FDA's 19 district offices located throughout the United States we responsible for the day-to-day monitoring of the recalls. We then used t information to determine, among other things, the number of recalls initia per year; the number of recalls by recall classification levels, the aver length of time from initiation to termination for recalls that were termin and the number and percentage of recalls by medical specialty of the de being recalled.

To assess the reliability of the information FDA provided, we rev FDA's user guide for RES and interviewed officials responsible for er and reviewing the information in RES. Additionally, for a sample of we compared information from RES on the status and key dates to the documents contained in FDA's recall files. We determined the data were sufficiently reliable for the purpose of our review. However, there are some limitations to our analyses. The data FDA provided may not include all recalls that firms actually initiated over this period. This is because FDA is dependent on firms self-reporting most recalls. In addition, FDA did not consistently enter certain data elements into RES over the 5-year period. For example, in certain cases the dates recalls were terminated were missing, and in many cases the root cause, or problem creating the need for the recall, was entered inconsistently. Therefore, we could not conduct certain analyses for all recalls initiated over the study period.

In addition to identifying information about the numbers and characteristics of recalls, we identified the extent to which FDA uses recall information to aid its oversight of recalls. To accomplish this, we interviewed officials from FDA's Office of Regulatory Affairs (ORA), which develops FDA-wide policy on compliance and enforcement matters and also has rimary responsibility for RES, the day-to-day monitoring of individual calls, and conducting inspections of firms. We also interviewed officials n FDA's Center for Devices and Radiological Health (CDRH), which lates medical devices marketed in the United States and is responsible for fying recalls and assessing the adequacy of a firm's actions to correct ns leading to the most serious recalls. In addition, we interviewed tatives from two device manufacturer associations and several device turers to obtain their views about the recall process.

entify the extent to which the medical device recall process ensures e implementation and termination of the highest-risk device recalls, d key documentation related to the recalling firms' management versight of a sample of the highest-risk recalls. We identified 131 d over the 5-year period to which FDA assigned its highest-risk recalls for which FDA determined that there was a reasonable the use of or exposure to the devices would cause serious nsequence or death. Of these 131, we selected a sample of 53 review by identifying the four FDA district offices that had of available recall files to review. These 53 recalls recalls during the 5-year period that were managed by for which there were files available for our review. For tained from FDA and reviewed the recall case files that rict offices. These files contained key documents such irms on the causes of the recalls, the firms' actions to ilar problems, the recall notifications firms sent out to customers, FDA's correspondence with firms, and documentation from RES. As part of our review, we identified actions recalling firms took to adhere to FDA's guidance and regulatory requirements, and the extent to which the firms were able to recall all of the affected devices. We also identified whether FDA followed its own procedures for overseeing and terminating the recalls and whether FDA's recall process was in conformance with internal control standards for the federal government.[8] For example, we reviewed the case files to determine whether or not FDA conducted recall audit checks in which FDA would contact a percentage of parties affected by the recall to determine whether they received the recall notice and followed the firms' instructions for removing or correcting the device. This included a review of over 2,000 audits check forms FDA completed for the 53 recalls we reviewed. Between December 2010 and February 2011 we discussed the recalls with officials from the responsible FDA district office, and determined the current status of the recalls.

We conducted this performance audit from January 2010 to June 2011, in accordance with generally accepted government auditing standards. Those standards require that we plan and perform the audit to obtain sufficient, appropriate evidence to provide a reasonable basis for our findings and conclusions based on our audit objectives. We believe that the evidence obtained provides a reasonable basis for our findings and conclusions based on our audit objectives.

BACKGROUND

FDA is responsible for ensuring that medical products—including medical devices—sold in the United States provide reasonable assurance of safety and effectiveness and do not pose a threat to public health. FDA's oversight responsibilities for medical devices begin before a product is brought to market and continue after a product is available for sale. Its premarket responsibilities include reviewing thousand of submissions for new devices filed each year to decide whether they should be allowed to be marketed in the United States. Its postmarket responsibilities include monitoring the safety of thousands of medical devices already on the market and identifying, analyzing and acting on potential risks the devices may pose to the public. Thi monitoring includes overseeing recalls of medical devices.

FDA's Classification and Approval or Clearance of Medical Devices

FDA classifies each device type into one of three classes—class I, II, or III—based on the level of risk it poses and the controls necessary to provide reasonable assurance of its safety and effectiveness. According to FDA, the risk the type of device poses to the user is a major factor in the class it is assigned: class I includes devices with the lowest risk, and class III includes devices with the highest risk. Examples of types of devices in each class include the following:

- class I: tongue depressors, elastic bandages, reading glasses, and forceps;
- class II: electrocardiographs, powered bone drills, and mercury thermometers; and
- class III: pacemakers and replacement heart valves.

In general, unless exempt under FDA regulations, medical devices are subject to one of two types of FDA premarket review before they may be legally marketed in the United States.[9] These reviews are as follows.

- **Premarket approval (PMA):** The manufacturer must submit evidence, typically including clinical data, providing reasonable assurance that the new device is safe and effective. The PMA process is the most stringent type of premarket review. A successful submission results in FDA's approval to market the device.
- **Premarket notification (510(k)):** Premarket notification is commonly called "510(k)" in reference to section 510(k) of the Federal Food, Drug, and Cosmetic Act where the notification requirement is listed. Under this review, the manufacturer must demonstrate to FDA that the new device is substantially equivalent to device already legally on the market.[10] For most 510(k) bmissions, clinical data are not required and substantial equivalence normally be determined based on comparative descriptions of a ce's intended use and technological characteristics, and may le performance data.[11] A successful submission results in FDA's ce to market the device.

Most class I device types and some class II devices are exempt from FDA's premarket review. In general, those that are not exempt, but which are substantially equivalent to a legally marked class I or class II device, are subject to premarket review through the 510(k) process. Class III device types are generally required to obtain FDA approval through the more stringent PMA process.[12]

The Voluntary Medical Device Recall Process

FDA defines a recall as a firm's removal or correction of a marketed product that FDA (1) considers to be in violation of the laws it administers, and (2) against which the agency would initiate legal action.[13] Nearly all medical device recalls are voluntarily initiated by a firm, usually the manufacturer of the device. The recall process generally consists of a series of steps that we have categorized into broad phases—initiating and classifying the recall, conducting and overseeing the recall, and completing and terminating the recall. While the recalling firm has primary responsibility for ensuring that the recalled devices are corrected or removed, FDA and other stakeholders each have responsibilities which they are supposed to undertake in order to effectively implement the various phases of a recall. FDA's role is generally to oversee a firm's management of recalls. It conducts its responsibilities as part of its postmarket surveillance. FDA staff from ORA—which is the lead office for all FDA field activities, including the agency's district offices—and CDRH are involved in overseeing recalls. Other stakeholders, including the firm's customers—such as distributors—and device users—such as hospitals or patients—are expected to correct or remove the recalled device according to the recalling firm's instructions.[14] A given recall may require the cooperation of thousands of different stakeholders depending on how many entities received, purchased, or used the device.

The following sections generally describe the voluntary recall process that FDA, as well as recalling firms, their customers, and device users, are expected to follow according to FDA's regulations, procedures, and guidance.

Initiating and Classifying the Recall

During this phase of a device recall, a firm initiates a recall, while FDA classifies the recall based on health risks presented by use of the device. As part of this phase, a firm develops a strategy for implementing the recall, and FDA reviews and suggests changes to the strategy. In most cases, a firm arrives at the decision to initiate a recall after discovering a problem with a device, or a series of similar devices.[15] The firm may then contact an FDA district office or immediately begin implementing a recall.[16] A firm may initiate a recall—that is notify stakeholders such as distributors and device users about the recall—prior to contacting the FDA district office. However, according to federal regulations, a firm must provide FDA with a report of correction or removal within 10 working days of initiating a recall of a product that involves or may involve a risk to health.[17] As part of its report, the firm is to provide FDA with key information such as the reason the device is being recalled, the brand name and model of the device, the lot or serial numbers of the device, the number of devices subject to correction or removal, and contact information for its customers and device users who received, used, or purchased the device. According to FDA's guidance, the recalling firm is also asked to develop a recall strategy that takes into account its assessment of the health hazard associated with the device. The strategy should contain details on the firm's plan for ensuring that its customers and device users correct or remove the device according to the firm's instructions, and the need for public warnings about the device. As part of its oversight, FDA will review the strategy, and may suggest that the firm make changes to its approach for conducting the recall.

Once the district office is notified about the recall, it should create a record in RES, notify CDRH, and obtain and evaluate information CDRH needs to make its classification decision. The district office monitoring the recall will provide any information it receives from the firm, including the correction and removal report, to CDRH so it can begin the process of classifying the recall. For some recalls, the district office may need to conduct a recall inspection at the establishment where the device is manufactured in order to obtain additional information needed to classify the recall. According to FDA's procedures, when a recall appears to involve significant health risks, an inspection should be conducted to determine, among other things, the root causes of the problem and if the firm is implementing appropriate corrective action. The inspection may be performed by the FDA district office monitoring the recall or other district offices, such as those located near the firm's manufacturing establishment.

To classify the recall, CDRH is to conduct its own health risk assessment of the device being recalled. Based on this assessment, CDRH classifies the recall to indicate the relative degree of health hazard presented by use of the device. According to CDRH's procedures, the classification decision should be completed within 31 calendar days from the time it received the information from the district office.[18] Recalls are classified into one of three categories:

- class I—reasonable probability that the use of, or exposure to, a device will cause serious adverse health consequences or death. These are the most serious recalls.
- class II—use of or exposure to a device may cause temporary or medically reversible adverse health consequences, or the probability of serious adverse health consequences is remote.
- class III—use of, or exposure to, a device is not likely to cause adverse health consequences.[19]

Table 1 compares FDA's classification of medical devices and recalls according to risk. It is important to note that FDA's device and recall classification schemes carry opposite designations. The potential degree of health risk associated with device classes is designated from class III (high) to class I (low), while the potential risk associated with recall classes is designated from class I (high) to class III (low).

Once the recall is classified, FDA is to notify the firm, in writing, of the assigned recall classification. This classification letter should also include instructions about the extent to which the firm should conduct effectiveness checks—that is, contacting customers and device users to determine whether the recall notification was received and acted upon appropriately. In general, for class I recalls, FDA recommends that firms conduct effectiveness checks with 100 percent of customers and device users affected by the recall. For class II recalls, FDA recommends effectiveness checks with 10 percent of such customers and device users, and 2 percent for class III recalls.

Table 1. Comparison of FDA Medical Device Classification and Recall Classification Levels, by Risk

Risk	Device classification	Recall classification
High	III	I
Moderate	II	II
Low	I	III

Source: GAO analysis of FDA classification information.

Conducting and Overseeing the Recall

During this phase, the firm and recall stakeholders are supposed to implement the recall as outlined in the approved recall strategy, and FDA is responsible for monitoring the progress made. Once a recall is under way, the firm is to conduct effectiveness checks to ensure that those stakeholders affected by the recall have received notification about the recall and have taken appropriate action, such as returning defective devices, or taking actions to correct the known defects. (See app. I for information on tools to help customers and medical device users identify recalled devices and an FDA initiative intended to better track devices through the use of unique identifiers.) Additionally, at the request of the FDA district office responsible for monitoring the recall, the firm is expected to provide status reports on the progress of the recall. These reports should include information on how many customers and device users have received the recall notification and followed the firm's instructions, and how many still need to respond to the recall notice. The FDA district office reviews the reports, and, using RES, assigns the recall a status of ongoing if the reports indicate the recall is still under way.

During the recall, FDA district offices independently assess the effectiveness of the recall by conducting audit checks.[20] According to the agency's procedures, for each check, investigative staff from one or more of FDA's district offices will contact individual distributors or device users. These audit checks are generally conducted in person or by telephone, to confirm that the distributor or device user (1) received notification from the firm about the recall and (2) properly corrected or removed the recalled devices in accordance with the firm's recall strategy. The FDA district office responsible for monitoring the recall assigns the audit checks to one or more of the district offices, depending upon the location of the firm's customers and the device users. According to FDA procedures, the district office monitoring the recall should assign audit checks within 10 days of the recalling firm's initiation of the recall. The audit checks should be completed by FDA investigators, if possible, within 10 days of assignment. If an investigator determines that the firm and the distributor or device user followed the recall strategy, the investigator's audit check should conclude that the recall was effective. If not, the investigator's audit check should conclude that the recall was ineffective. The result of the audit check is documented on a standardized FDA form, and each form is provided to the district office that made the audit check assignment.

Completing and Terminating the Recall

Once the firm believes it has completed the recall—i.e., done everything as outlined in the recall strategy—it needs to submit a final recall status report/recall termination request to the FDA district office monitoring the recall.[21] Regardless of the class of the recall, if the district office agrees that the firm has completed the recall, it is to change the status of the recall in RES to completed. If it disagrees, it generally requests the firm to take additional actions, such as re-contacting customers and device users. The FDA district office bases its assessment of whether the recall has been effectively completed by reviewing the firm's status reports and results of the audit checks. In addition, according to FDA procedures, the final monitoring step the district office may take is to conduct a limited postrecall inspection to verify that the recall has been completed. During this inspection, investigators should witness destruction or reconditioning of the recalled product, if applicable.

Once the district office considers a recall completed, FDA assesses whether it can terminate a recall. As part of its assessment, FDA may review a corrective and preventive action plan submitted by the recalling firm that describes the firm's actions to prevent a recurrence of the problem that led to the recall. Thus, this phase of the recall process is important because it provides FDA with the opportunity to determine whether the firm has taken sufficient corrective and preventive actions. The agency's procedures state that if a firm's corrective and preventive actions are adequate, FDA staff should terminate a recall within 3 months of completion. When terminating a class I recall, the district office sends a recall termination recommendation to CDRH. CDRH reviews the recalling firm's corrective and preventive action plan, and effectiveness and audit check results, and makes the decision on whether to terminate the recall. The district office does not need CDRH approval to terminate class II and III recalls. If corrective actions are determined sufficient, the recall status in RES is changed from completed to terminated. When FDA terminates a recall, the district office will close the recall file and notify the firm, in writing, that it can cease recall activity. Figure 1 displays the general process from initiating to terminating a recall.

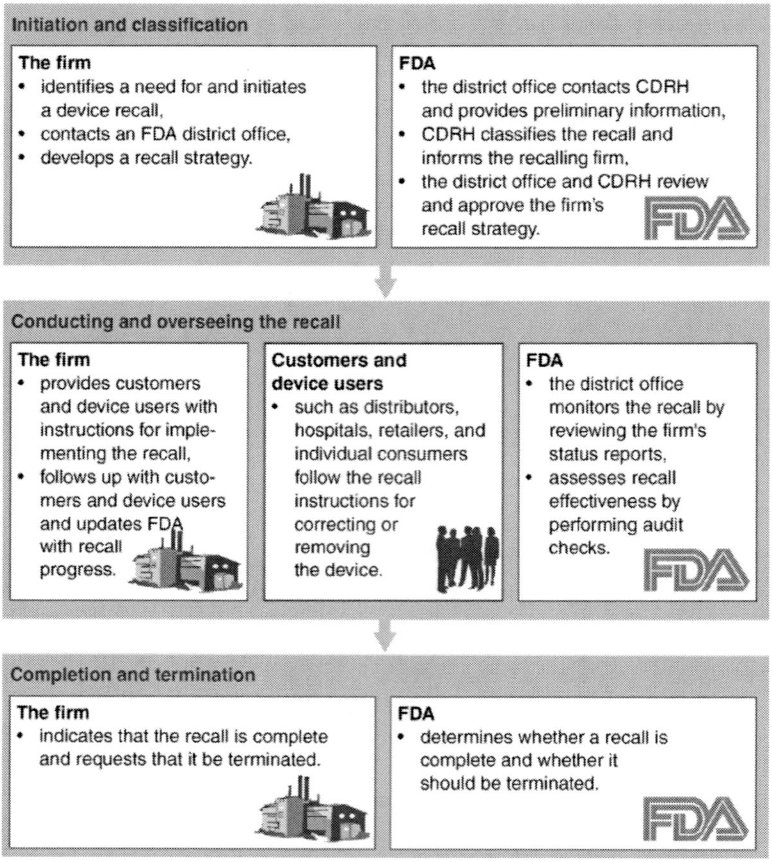

Source: GAO analysis of FDA information.

Note: According to FDA officials, the various phases of the recall process may not necessarily occur sequentially, and individual actions may be occurring simultaneously in different phases of the process for specific recalls.

Figure 1. The Voluntary Medical Device Recall Process Followed by FDA, Firms, Customers, and Device Users.

FIRMS INITIATED SEVERAL THOUSAND MEDICAL DEVICE RECALLS, BUT FDA HAS NOT ROUTINELY ANALYZED THIS INFORMATION TO AID ITS OVERSIGHT OF RECALLS

From 2005 through 2009, firms initiated 3,510 medical device recalls. Most of these were for medical devices in five areas of use or medical specialty areas. On average, the recall process took just over 420 days from initiation to termination, with class I recalls (the highest-risk recalls) averaging nearly 520 days. FDA has not routinely analyzed information about recalls to aid its oversight of the recall process, and thus could not explain trends in recalls over this time period.

Several Thousand Device Recalls Were Initiated; Most Were Class II and Involved Cardiovascular and Radiological Devices

Between January 1, 2005, and December 31, 2009, firms initiated 3,510 device recalls, an average of just over 700 per year. The annual volume fluctuated over this period, and ranged from a low of 658 in 2006 to a high of 796 in 2008. FDA classified the vast majority of all recalls—nearly 83 percent—as class II, meaning use of these devices may cause temporary adverse health consequences (moderate risk).

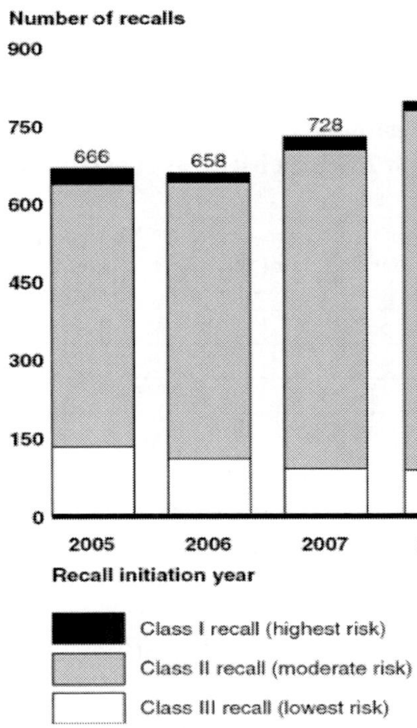

Source: GAO analysis of FDA data.

Figure 2. Number of Medical Device Recalls Initiated from 2005 through 2009.

FDA classified 14 percent as class III, meaning use of the device is not likely to cause any adverse consequences (lowest risk); and 4 percent were classified as class I (highest risk), because FDA determined that there was a reasonable probability that the use of or exposure to a violative product would cause serious adverse health consequences or death (see figure 2). The number of class I recalls initiated between 2005 and 2009 ranged from 17 to 41. For example, in 2007, 25 class I recalls were initiated; in 2008, 17 were initiated; and in 2009, 41 were initiated. In comparison, the number of class II recalls generally increased each year and consistently exceeded 500 annually.

Our analysis found that approximately 60 percent of recalls during this period were for devices from five areas of use or medical specialty areas—cardiovascular, radiological, orthopedic, general hospital and personal use, and diagnostic chemistry.[22] According to FDA, these medical specialties are among those with the greatest number of devices on the market and four of the five specialties—cardiovascular, radiological, orthopedic, and general hospital—account for the greatest number of devices cleared or approved for marketing each year. The remaining recalls were for devices in 19 other areas (such as general and plastic surgery and neurological devices); no other specialty accounted for more than 8 percent of recalls (see table 2).

Table 2. Number and Percentage of Medical Device Recalls Initiated from 2005 through 2009, by Medical Specialty Area

Medical specialty area	Total number of recalls	Percentage of all recalls	Number of class I recalls[a]	Percentage of class I recalls
Cardiovascular	532	15	40	31
Radiological	484	14	2	2
Orthopedic	410	12	4	3
General hospital and personal use[b]	388	11	31	24
Diagnostic chemistry[c]	315	9	16	12
Other specialty areas	1,381	39	38	29
Total	**3,510**	**100**	**131**	**100**

Source: GAO analysis of FDA data.

Note: Percentages do not add to 100 percent due to rounding.

[a] Class I recalls involve a reasonable probability that the use of, or exposure to, a device will cause serious adverse health consequences or death.

[b] General hospital and personal use devices include bandages, examination gowns, and stretchers.

[c] Diagnostic chemistry devices include test systems, such as those for measuring blood glucose.

As table 2 shows, for class I recalls, the greatest numbers were for devices from the cardiovascular medical specialty. In addition, the table shows that devices from the general hospital and personal use and diagnostic chemistry medical specialties accounted for a substantial number of class I recalls. Among class I recalls, we found that the largest number for cardiovascular devices involved automatic external defibrillators. The largest number of recalls for general hospital and personal use devices involved infusion pumps, including implantable programmable pumps.

Table 3. Number and Percentage of Medical Device Recalls Initiated During 2008 and 2009, by Root Cause

FDA assigned root cause[a]	Total number of recalls	Percentage of all recalls	Number of class I recalls[b]	Percentage of class I recalls
Process control[c]	233	16	17	29
Device design	201	14	12	21
Software design	181	12	1	2
Component design/selection	59	4	7	12
Additional root causes[d]	782	53	21	36
Total	**1,456**	**100**	**58**	**100**

Source: GAO analysis of FDA data.

[a] The root cause is the problem creating a need for the recall.

[b] Class I recalls involve a reasonable probability that the use of, or exposure to, a device will cause serious adverse health consequences or death.

[c] Process control entails developing, conducting, controlling, and monitoring production processes to ensure that a device conforms to its specifications.

[d] Other root causes include false or misleading labeling, mistaken use of materials or components, or employee error.

RES also contains information on the root cause of recalls, that is, the problem creating a need for the recall. On average, in 2008 and 2009 (the only years for which FDA tracked these data in RES) the greatest numbers of recalls were caused by problems with manufacturing processes. FDA refers to this root cause as process control—developing, conducting, controlling, and monitoring production processes to ensure that a device conforms to its specifications. Other leading causes were device design and software design. The two most common causes of class I recalls were the same as for all classes—process control and device design—but the third cause was component design or selection (see table 3). In general, FDA officials indicated they do not believe that there is a relationship between root cause and recall class. However, FDA officials indicated that some root causes of recalls are more likely to affect certain types of devices. For example, they stated that the root cause "incorrect or missing expiration date" is typically related to devices that involve sterilization.

Among all classes of recalls, we found that a higher proportion of recalls were for devices which were cleared for market through the 510(k) process as compared to other FDA review processes. This reflects the fact that the overwhelming majority of devices—99 percent, according to FDA—enter the market through this review process. Our analysis of RES data for 2,773 recalls[23] found that 87 percent of recalls involved a device cleared through the 510(k) process, nearly 8 percent involved a device approved through the more stringent PMA or PMA supplement process, and nearly 6 percent involved devices that were cleared through the 510(k) process and approved through the PMA process, or that were exempt from FDA review.[24]

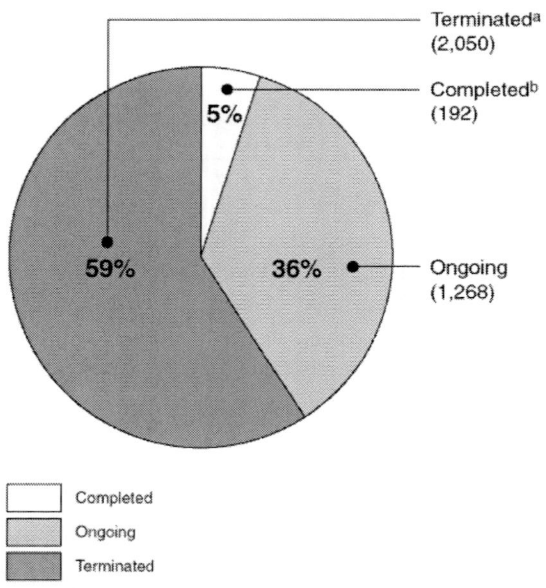

Source: GAO analysis of FDA data.

Note: Status as of April 16, 2010.

[a] Terminated—FDA headquarters determined that firms' corrective actions taken were sufficient to prevent a recurrence of the problems that led to the recall.

[b] Completed—An FDA district office concluded that the firm had essentially fulfilled their responsibilities for correcting or removing the devices.

Figure 3. Status of Medical Device Recalls Initiated from 2005 through 2009.

We found similar trends for 101 class I recalls.[25] We found that 74 of the recalls (73 percent) were for devices cleared through the 510(k) process, 22 percent were for PMA-approved devices, and the remaining 5 percent involved devices that were cleared through the 510(k) process and approved through the PMA process, or that were exempt from FDA review.[26] Compared to all recall classes, a higher percentage of class I recalls involved devices cleared through the PMA process (22 percent compared with 8 percent for all classes of recalls combined), which likely reflects the high risk of these devices.

Additionally, we found that 14 of those 74 class I recalls involving devices that were cleared through the 510(k) process were for devices that FDA designated as high-risk devices—class III devices. We further found that all 14 recalls involved cardiovascular devices, including 12 for automatic external defibrillators.

FDA Has Terminated Most Medical Device Recalls, with the Recall Process Taking over 500 Days for the Highest-Risk Recalls

At the time of our review, the 3,510 medical device recalls initiated from 2005 through 2009 were in various stages of the recall process. Approximately 60 percent—2,050—of all recalls initiated in this period had been terminated by FDA as of April 16, 2010, the date we received data from FDA. Firms had completed another 5 percent and were awaiting FDA's review and decision on termination. The remaining 36 percent were ongoing (see figure 3).

We found that for recalls that had been terminated, the time between the firm's initiation and FDA's termination of a recall varied by class.[27] On average, over 420 days passed between initiation of a recall and FDA's termination. Among all classes of recalls, class I recalls took the longest—on average 516 days, while on average class II recalls took 436 days and class III took 352 days.[28] The amount of time needed to conduct and terminate recalls was split roughly evenly between the portions of the process that are primarily the recalling firms' responsibilities—conducting the recall itself—and the portions that are primarily FDA's responsibility—oversight of the recall (see figure 4).

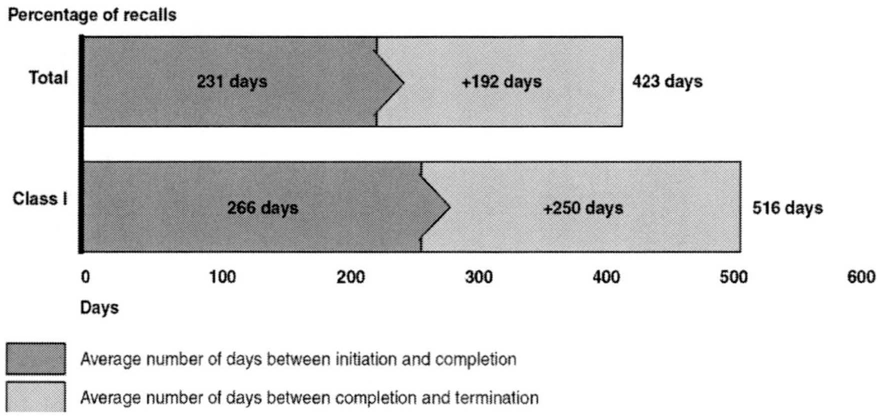

Source: GAO analysis of FDA data.

Note: Termination dates were available for 2,028 of the 2,050 recalls that were terminated during this period.

Figure 4. Average Time from Initiation to Termination for Medical Device Recalls Initiated from 2005 through 2009.

FDA frequently did not meet its 3 month time frame for terminating completed recalls. It did not meet this time frame for more than half of all recalls and over 70 percent of class I recalls (see figure 5). On average, FDA took 192 days to terminate a recall after it determined a recall was completed, more than twice the time specified in its procedures. For class I recalls, the average was 250 days. FDA could not specifically identify reasons that explained why it took this amount of time to make termination decisions. The agency did indicate that termination time frames are affected by both FDA's ability to address recalling firms' termination requests, as well as firms' ability to provide adequate information in support of the termination decision. This information may include a sufficient corrective and preventive action plan to prevent a recurrence of the problem which led to the recall. These data indicate that the timeliness of recall termination decisions appears to have deteriorated since our 1998 report.[29]

At the time of our review, 36 percent—1,268 recalls—were ongoing. Of these, most had been initiated in the past few years; however, some have been ongoing since 2005, the beginning of our review period. Of those recalls that were ongoing, most were initiated in 2008 and 2009; however, 456 (36 percent) had been ongoing for at least 2 years, including 86 that had been ongoing for nearly 5 years.

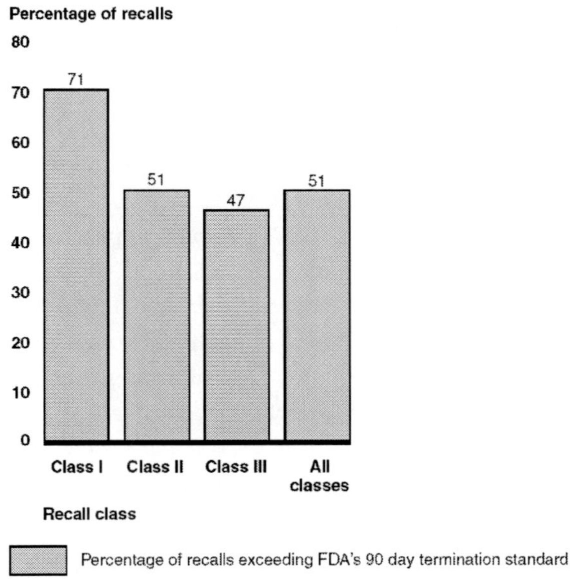

Source: GAO analysis of FDA data.

Note: Completion and termination dates were available for 1,992 of the 2,050 recalls that were terminated. A recall is considered complete when FDA agrees that the recalling firm has sufficiently completed all recall-related activities. A recall is terminated when FDA determines that in addition to completing the recall, the recalling firm has taken adequate corrective measures to prevent a recurrence of issues which led to the recall.

Figure 5. Percentage of Medical Device Recalls Terminated More Than 90 Days after Completion Date, for Recalls Initiated in Calendar Years 2005 through 2009.

FDA Has Not Routinely Analyzed Data to Identify Systemic Problems Underlying Device Recalls

Although RES contains numerous data elements that would allow for analyses of recall data, FDA is not effectively using these data to identify whether there are systemic problems underlying recalls.[30] Instead of using RES to conduct systemic analyses of recalls, which would be consistent with one of the agency's strategic goals—improving the quality and safety of manufactured products in the supply chain—FDA has used RES primarily for processing and tracking the progress of individual recalls.

Agency officials have not been using RES as a management tool to conduct broad surveillance of recalls and related issues. Neither the district offices we contacted nor CDRH officials prepared routine reports that would enable officials to identify areas of potential concern in the recall process, such as recalls that have been ongoing for an extended period, or whether specific manufacturing or design problems are causing increases in recalls or the types of devices being recalled. In fact, FDA officials appeared to be unaware of RES's capability to generate summary data. When we requested data from RES, FDA staff were unable to extract these data themselves, and initially indicated that it would be impossible to obtain data from RES. After 2 months, FDA officials concluded that through a special arrangement with a contractor they could obtain the RES data and meet our request.

After we completed our analysis of the RES data, we provided key summaries to FDA officials, and asked them to comment on trends that we observed. Officials indicated that they have not fully analyzed these data and could not explain trends without extensive research of individual case files. They indicated that at most, they could offer speculation about some of the trends we observed. For example, they could not explain why the majority of recalls are class II, why class I recalls more than doubled between 2008 and 2009, or why many recalls had been ongoing for 5 years. Officials also could not provide definitive answers when we asked them to comment on other related topics, such as:

- common causes of recalls;
- trends in the number of recalls over time;
- variation in the numbers of recalls by recall classification levels;
- types of devices and medical specialties of devices accounting for most recalls;
- the length of time needed for firms to complete recalls; and
- the length of time needed for FDA to terminate recalls.

Although FDA has not been routinely analyzing recall data to identify whether there are systemic problems affecting recalls, officials indicated they have used these data to help direct their inspection resources, and to support compliance and enforcement actions. First, FDA officials indicated they use recall information as one of many elements to assess the relative risks that device manufacturers present, and thus which firms the agency should inspect in a given year. For example, the officials said that recall data is one of several elements that feed into a predictive model that determines the likelihood that firms are out of compliance with applicable laws or regulations, and therefore in need of inspection. Second, they told us they have plans to use recall information as the basis for developing a directed inspection plan. As part of this project, officials would use recall information to identify those firms that generate a large number of recalls, and target them for inspection. Officials indicated that these inspections would focus on specific areas—such as a particular manufacturing process. This effort is still in the planning phase, and officials have not yet established criteria, such as what constitutes a large number of recalls, for determining which firms to select. The officials also indicated that progress may be slow because they do not have sufficient resources available to devote to this effort.[31]

Although FDA has not regularly been using data to identify systemic problems, we found one example of FDA using recall data to detect and address safety issues with a particular type of device. In December 2010, FDA held a conference on a variety of issues related to automatic external defibrillators, including the safety of these devices. During this conference it presented historical recall data to help demonstrate the need for a specific focus on safety improvements for this type of device.[32]

GAPS IN THE MEDICAL DEVICE RECALL PROCESS LIMIT THE EFFECTIVE IMPLEMENTATION AND TERMINATION OF THE HIGHEST-RISK RECALLS

Gaps in the medical device recall process limit firms' and FDA's ability to ensure that the highest-risk recalls are implemented effectively and terminated in a timely manner. We found that both FDA and recalling firms generally upheld their respective responsibilities in the course of initiating and classifying recalls. However, FDA did not always follow its own procedures and some procedures are unclear. FDA did not consistently inspect the manufacturing establishments of recalling firms as outlined in the agency's procedures. FDA has also not established criteria, such as thresholds, based on the nature of devices, for assessing whether firms effectively completed recalls by correcting or removing a sufficient number of recalled devices. Further, we found that firms face challenges, such as locating specific devices or users of devices, and often could not correct or remove all devices. We also found that audit checks, a key mechanism for FDA's oversight of firms' conduct of recalls, are limited in scope. In addition, because of a lack of clarity in FDA's audit check procedures, they have been implemented inconsistently by FDA's district offices. Finally, FDA frequently failed to make recall termination decisions in a timely manner, and kept no documentation to justify its termination decisions.

Firms and FDA Have Generally Implemented Recalls Appropriately in the Initiation and Classification Phases, but FDA Has Failed to Consistently Conduct Recall-Related Inspections

In our review of a sample of the highest-risk device recalls initiated from January 1, 2005, through December 31, 2009, we found that once firms initiated recalls, they generally provided FDA with a correction or removal report in a timely manner—within FDA's 10-day time frame. In 51 of the 53 recalls (96 percent), firms submitted a correction or removal report to FDA. For 43 of these 51 recalls, firms submitted the report within 10 working days of initiating the recall. For 6 of the remaining 8 recalls, the correction and removal report was submitted within 21 business days; the reports for the other 2 recalls were submitted 62 business days and 227 business days after the recall was initiated, respectively. Table 4 shows the proportion of recalls, by district, where firms submitted these reports and whether they were submitted within 10 working days.

Table 4. Number, Percentage, and Timeliness of Correction or Removal Reports Submitted for a Sample of Class I Medical Device Recalls Initiated from 2005 through 2009, by FDA District

District office	Number Of recalls	Number of Correction or removal Reports submitted	Percentage Of correction or removal reports submitted	Number of correction or removal reports submitted within 10 working days	Percentage of correction or removal Reports submitted within10 working days
Detroit	9	9	100	8	89
Los Angeles	15	14	93	9	64
Minneapolis	16	16	100	15	94
New England	13	12	92	11	92
Total	**53**	**51**	**96**	**43**	**84**

Source: GAO analysis of FDA medical device recall files.

Although our analysis indicates that firms generally provided these reports after initiating the recalls, FDA officials cautioned that this does not mean firms fully complied with the regulatory reporting requirements. They indicated that in some cases, firms' initial correction or removal reports lack some of the information needed and extra time was required for firms to provide additional information. To help address this, officials indicated that in November 2010 they began a recall process improvement project. As part of this initiative, CDRH plans to develop Web-based training modules for industry clarifying the information that needs to be provided when reporting corrections and removals to FDA.[33]

FDA infrequently—in less than one-half of the recalls—conducted an establishment inspection upon learning of a recall. According to FDA's procedures, upon learning of a potential class I recall, district offices should conduct establishment inspections to obtain further information about the recall. We found that FDA conducted such recall-related inspections for 20 of the 53 class I recalls we reviewed.[34] The frequency of inspections varied across the four district offices monitoring the recalls. Three of these offices (Detroit, Los Angeles, and New England) conducted recall-related establishment inspections upon the initiation of a recall between 25 percent and 38 percent of the time, while the Minneapolis district office conducted them in 62 percent of recalls (see figure 6). Based on interviews with FDA officials in four district offices, we found that decisions to conduct such inspections, given their overall inspection workload, are a matter of resources and timing. Some district officials also said that the decision to conduct a recall-related inspection is based on the firm's recall history and indicated that FDA may be less likely to inspect a firm with a history of completing recalls successfully. Finally, some of these officials FDA said that this is because firms that have successfully completed recalls generally provide the necessary information, such as determinations of the root cause of the recall, as part of their correction or removal reports.

FDA generally followed its procedures by classifying each of the 53 recalls in our sample and providing written notification to the recalling firms. However, for 28 of the 53 recalls, FDA did not make its classification determination within 31days as outlined in its procedures.[35] The amount of time from recall initiation to classification varied, ranging from a few days to several months, with an average of 47 days.

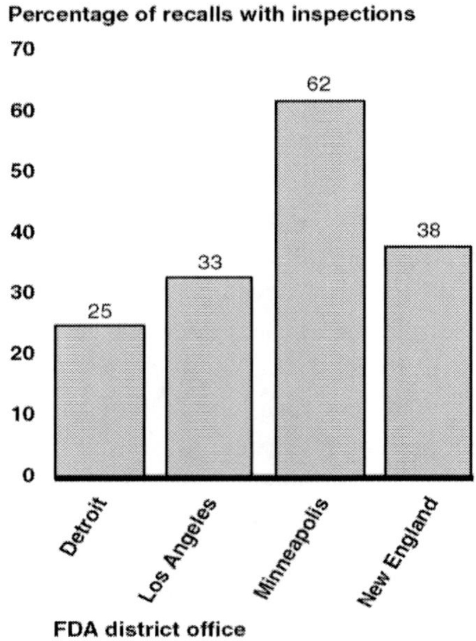

Source: GAO analysis of FDA medical device recall files.

Note: We selected a sample of 53 recalls for in-depth review by identifying the four FDA district offices that had the largest number of available recall files to review. This figure includes 49 of the 53 recalls in our sample of class I recalls. FDA identified the problem that led to the remaining 4 recalls—1 from the Detroit and 3 from the Minneapolis district offices—through postmarket establishment inspections, unrelated to recalls. Therefore, FDA did not conduct additional inspections upon the initiation of these recalls.

Figure 6. Percentage of Our Sample of Class I Medical Device Recalls Initiated from 2005 through 2009 for Which Recall-Related Inspections Were Conducted, by FDA District Office.

Representatives from two device manufacturer associations and several device manufacturers expressed concern about the length of time it can take FDA to classify recalls. For a class I recall, firms must make greater efforts to identify and contact customers than for class II recalls. Thus, delays in FDA's classification can affect firms' decisions. For example, officials indicated that if they send out a recall notice that they believe will be a class II, and after a significant amount of time FDA informs them it is a class I recall, the firm will have to revise the notice to indicate that the risks posed by the recall were more severe than they initially anticipated. The firm will also have to identify additional customers and device users to contact, in order to meet FDA's recommendation that they conduct 100 percent effectiveness checks for class I recalls. Firm officials said that they will then send out the revised notice, which can create confusion about whether this is a new recall or whether it is an update with new instructions for the already ongoing recall.

Firms Faced Challenges in Correcting or Removing All Recalled Devices

Our review of firms' action in conducting recalls found that the status of recalls varied and that firms face challenges in correcting or removing all recalled products.

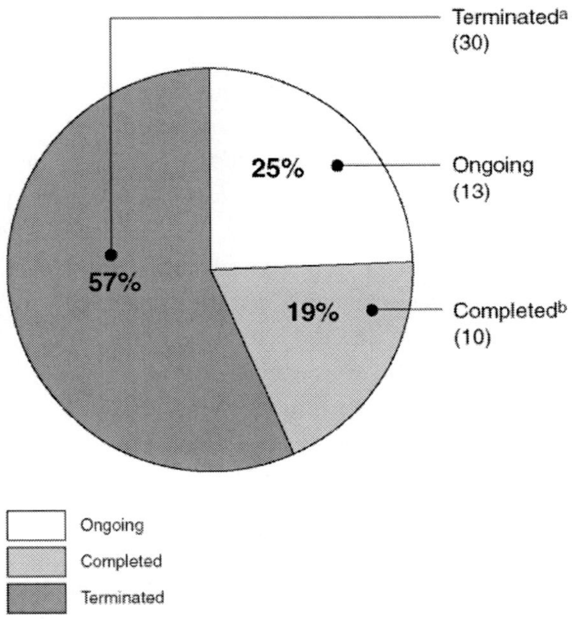

Source: GAO analysis of FDA medical device rec all files.

Note: We obtained the current status of these recalls through our reviews of FDA's recall files and discussions with FDA district office officials between December 2010 and February 2011. Percentages may not sum to 100 because of rounding.

[a] Terminated—FDA headquarters determined that firms' corrective actions taken were sufficient to prevent a recurrence of the problems that let to the recall.

[b] Completed—An FDA district office concluded that the firm had essentially fulfilled their responsibilities for correcting or removing the devices.

Figure 7. Status of Our Sample of 53 Class I Medical Device Recalls Initiated from 2005 through 2009.

Of the 53 recalls we reviewed, we found 13 were ongoing, 10 were completed—meaning that an FDA district office concluded that the firm had essentially fulfilled their responsibilities for correcting or removing the devices—and 30 were terminated—meaning FDA headquarters determined that firms' corrective actions taken were sufficient to prevent a recurrence of the problems that let to the recall (see figure 7).[36]

Of the 40 recalls in our sample that were either completed or terminated—meaning that FDA concluded that the firm had taken sufficient effort to correct or remove recalled devices—we found that for 19 (48 percent) of these recalls, firms were able to correct or remove all products. In the other 21 recalls (53 percent) firms were unable to correct or remove all products. These recalls ranged widely, in both volume of devices subject to recall and the types of devices being recalled. Some recalls involved hundreds of thousands of disposable products, while others involved a small number of life-sustaining implantable devices. Although recalling firms took steps to notify customers and device users, they were often unable to correct or remove all devices. This was because firms could not locate some of the customers or device users, or these customers or device users could not locate the device subject to recall. In other cases this was because the devices had been disposed of (such as defective syringes), or were sold at retail outlets (such as glucose test strips) to individuals who may not have known about the recall. For example, in a recall of tracheal tubes included in certain pediatric medical kits, 1,400 tubes had been distributed, but only 200 were returned to the recalling firm. The firm said that the rest had likely been used. Finally, users occasionally were unwilling to return a device. For example, one recall involved a magnetic device designed to treat a variety of medical problems such as lower back pain, fibromyalgia, and arthritis. This device was never cleared or approved by FDA, and despite FDA warnings about the device, users who had purchased units refused to return them. Details concerning the 21 recalls for which firms were not able to correct or remove all devices are presented in appendix II.

FDA's Oversight of Recalls Is Inconsistent and Narrow in Scope and Its Procedures Are Unclear

Our review of FDA's actions for conducting and overseeing recalls revealed that FDA generally conducted audit checks for the class I recalls we reviewed, but we found unclear procedures led to numerous inconsistencies in how different investigators conducted these checks and made their determinations about the effectiveness of recalls. FDA conducted audit checks for 45 of the 53 recalls (85 percent) we reviewed.[37] Our analysis of 2,196 audit check forms associated with these recalls found that audit checks completed for nearly 90 percent of the recalls contained a variety of inconsistencies in how the audit checks were implemented and documented.[38] For each of these recalls we found inconsistencies in how different investigators determined whether a recall was effective or ineffective when conducting their audit checks of recalls. We also identified inconsistencies in the level of detail provided in the audit check report, and the level of effort undertaken by different investigators. Specifically, we found the following.

- Some investigators' audit checks concluded that recalls were effective, despite noting problems (such as device users not following the firm's instructions), while other investigators concluded that similar instances were ineffective. For example, in 2008 a firm initiated a recall of an implantable pump because of problems in the connection between a catheter and the pump, which could result in improper amounts of medication being delivered to a patient. The firm's recall notification alerted physicians to this problem, and provided instructions for monitoring patients who already had the implanted pump and for revising future implant procedures. As part of the audit check program for this recall, FDA's investigators contacted a sample of physicians to determine whether they received the notification and followed the instructions. Our review found that out of 68 audit checks, there were 14 instances where the investigators noted that physicians either did not receive the recall notification, or did not remember receiving it, and thus could not have followed the recall notice instructions. In 8 of these 14 instances, investigators concluded that the recall was ineffective, noting that the physicians did not implement the recall instructions. In contrast, in the other 6 instances they concluded the recall was effective, even though physicians could not have followed the recall instructions. In some cases this was because the firm provided evidence that they had notified the physician, and in others the investigator noted that the physician did not have any pumps on hand.
- Some investigators determined that device users were not notified of the recall by the recalling firm, but instead learned of the recall through other means. In some of these instances, investigators' audit

checks concluded that recalls were effective, while in other similar cases investigators concluded the checks were ineffective.

- Some investigators wrote detailed comments on the audit check form as to why the investigator determined the recall was effective or ineffective, while others did not. Without comments, it may be difficult for FDA supervisors and district recall coordinators to verify whether an investigator correctly determined whether the recall was effective or ineffective.
- Some investigators noted actions they took when they discovered problems with recalls, such as providing the device users with a copy of the recall notice or instructing them on actions to take in order to implement a recall. In contrast, other investigators did not indicate whether they made any attempt to help facilitate the recall. For example, in 2009 a firm initiated a recall of an automated external defibrillator because of reports that some of these devices failed to discharge sufficient energy due to problems with batteries. The firm issued a notice that instructed users to replace batteries and update software for the devices. As part of the audit checks for this recall, FDA investigators contacted a sample of users of the device, to check whether they received the recall notification and followed the firm's recall instructions. Our review found that out of 67 audit checks, there were 35 instances where investigators noted problems with the recall—generally that the user did not receive the notice or failed to follow recall instructions. In 29 of these cases, the FDA investigator noted taking actions, including providing the recall notice or instructing the user to contact the recalling firm so they could obtain software needed to perform the needed actions. However, in 6 cases we found no indication that the FDA investigator took actions to ensure the recall was carried out effectively.

FDA officials at both ORA and the district offices we contacted acknowledged that there are no detailed instructions or requirements for conducting audit checks, and that there can be inconsistencies in the process. Officials told us that when determining whether or not a check is effective, investigators should be assessing whether the recalling firm provided the notice and instructions to the customers or device users, and whether the customers or users followed instructions. They acknowledged, however, that some investigators may approach these checks differently, and that this may be an area where clarification of the agency's procedures is needed. During our interviews with officials from the Detroit, Los Angeles, Minneapolis, and New England district offices, some officials said that audit checks are typically conducted by new investigators, and that investigators receive classroom and on-the-job training on how to conduct such checks. Some district officials also noted that audit checks are reviewed by a supervisor as well as the recall coordinator in the district office that is monitoring the recall, and this serves as a quality control function to ensure consistency. Also, officials from FDA headquarters and some district offices stated that they have attempted to institute measures to improve the audit check process. Specifically, they noted that they recently updated the audit check form to more precisely reflect what makes a recall ineffective. Also, ORA officials indicated that they plan to automate the audit check forms, which will make the forms accessible to officials in FDA's headquarters. FDA officials said that they are considering applications for analyzing the automated data, but have not completed any specific plans.

In addition to the inconsistencies, we found other gaps in FDA's oversight related to the audit checks. First, FDA's audit checks were often narrow in scope, in that FDA instructs investigators to contact only a small number of customers or device users—between 2 percent and 10 percent of those affected by the recall. Therefore, if there are thousands of customers or device users, the audit checks provide FDA with a means to contact a relatively small number of them. For the 45 recalls for which FDA completed checks, we found the number of audit checks conducted varied widely, from 2 to 271, with an average of 51 audit checks per recall.[39] Second, FDA investigators did not always conduct the assigned number of audit checks. We compared the number of audit checks that should have been conducted based on the audit check assignments to the numbers of checks actually completed. We found that for 17 of the 45 recalls (38 percent) fewer than the assigned number were conducted. Third, even though most checks were done in person, consistent with FDA's procedures, over 22 percent of the checks were done by telephone. In these cases, the audit check relied extensively on anecdotal information provided by the customer or device user. According to FDA, the number of checks it can perform is limited by available resources. Based on our review of files, we found that if patients or consumers are involved (e.g., if FDA needed to contact someone with an implantable device), these were often done by telephone. We also found checks that were done by telephone for other device users including hospitals, retailers, and doctors' offices.

Gaps in FDA's Completion and Termination Process Increase the Risk That Unsafe Medical Devices May Continue to be Used

We found FDA lacks specific criteria for making decisions about whether recalling firms have adequately completed their recalls—a key oversight activity of the recall process. FDA officials indicated they consider a recall complete when a firm has completed actions outlined in its recall strategy. In particular, they evaluate whether firms completed their assigned level of effectiveness checks, and have corrected or removed recalled devices in "an acceptable manner." However, our review of FDA's recall procedures found—and FDA officials confirmed—that the procedures do not contain any specific criteria or general guidelines governing the extent to which firms should be correcting or removing various types of devices before a recall should be considered completed. For example, FDA does not have a benchmark recovery rate or threshold to assess whether firms effectively completed recalls, although the recovery rates of devices could be expected to vary, depending on whether a recalled device was a large piece of hospital equipment or a disposable device, such as a syringe.

Representatives from medical device firms stated that there are no criteria or guidance from FDA on the percentage of recalled products that must be corrected or removed. Further, these firm representatives said that FDA is generally satisfied with three attempts at communicating with customers and device users affected by the recall.

In addition, for a majority of the class I recalls we reviewed, FDA's actions to ensure that recalls were complete were inconsistent with its procedures for overseeing recalls. According to FDA's procedures, districts should conduct a limited postrecall inspection to verify that the recall is complete, and to witness destruction of defective products, if applicable. In 21 of the 40 completed and terminated recalls (53 percent) we found no documented evidence that FDA took actions besides audit checks to verify that the recall was complete. In the other 48 percent of recalls, FDA made an assessment via inspection, witnessing destruction of devices, or verifying that software corrections were completed.

Another gap we found in the recall process is that FDA does not maintain sufficient documentation to justify its termination decisions. Although FDA may request that firms submit corrective and preventative action plans for review and approval before a recall can be terminated, we found little documentation on how FDA assessed whether such plans were sufficient when it terminated recalls. When we asked to review documentation justifying the decisions for the terminated recalls in our sample, FDA officials indicated that they do not maintain extensive documentation justifying the basis for their termination decisions. They told us that creating documentation to support concurrence with the termination recommendation is not part of past or current termination procedures. This approach is inconsistent with internal control standards for the federal government, which indicate "that all transactions and other significant events need to be clearly documented" and stress the importance of "the creation and maintenance of related records which provide evidence of execution of these activities as well as appropriate documentation."[40] Without such documentation, we were unable to assess the extent to which FDA's termination process appropriately evaluated recalling firms' corrective actions.

Also, we found that FDA termination decisions were frequently not made in a timely manner—within 3 months of the completion of the recall—increasing the risk that unsafe or defective devices remained available for use. Of the 53 files in our sample, 30 were terminated—meaning FDA headquarters determined that firms developed sufficient corrective actions to prevent a recurrence of problems which led to the recalls. For 73 percent of the terminated recalls, FDA did not make its termination decision within 3 months of the recall's completion, as indicated by FDA procedures. Overall, termination decisions took between 10 and 800 business days from completion to termination, with an average of 187 business days. Failure to make termination decisions in a timely manner increases the risk that patients and healthcare providers may continue to use unsafe or defective devices. For example, one firm requested termination from FDA for its recall of a portable external defibrillator in February 2006. However, FDA did not begin its termination assessment until May 2010. In this case, officials indicated that, due to staff turnover in the district office, they were unaware that this recall was still ongoing until a new recall coordinator searched for ongoing recalls. In 2010, following an FDA inquiry, the firm stated that it had not received confirmation of a required upgrade from 91 end users and an additional 13 devices could not be located. Because FDA did not follow up on this recall until 2010, 4 years had elapsed before the agency became aware that the recalling firm had not corrected or removed a substantial number of devices subject to the recall. According to FDA officials, their ability to terminate recalls in a timely manner is affected by resources, and termination decisions are a lower priority than other issues because the recalling firm has completed its actions.

We found at least one instance where FDA's failure to make a timely termination assessment allowed for a potentially unsafe product to be reintroduced into the market and used for surgical procedures. In this case, based on adverse event reports that screws in its spinal fixation system were becoming loose postoperatively, the firm decided to recall the device in December 2005. The firm implemented its recall and removed all devices. The firm indicated that it developed a corrective action for the screw problem, and relaunched the device in April 2006. It then requested termination from FDA in May 2006. FDA followed up on this request by leaving three voice mail messages with the firm, and received no response. The agency sent out a request for information a year later, in May 2007. In June 2007, the company again indicated that the recall was complete, and requested termination. In September 2007, FDA conducted an inspection of the company's manufacturing facility, and found that while the recall was complete, the corrective action was not adequate. Over the course of the next 2 years, the firm worked with FDA to get revisions to the device approved, but eventually agreed to a second recall for the revised device. This recall was initiated in May 2009. We identified five reports of adverse events related to continuing problems with the implanted device that were filed with FDA subsequent to the firm's relaunch of the device in April 2006. These reports were filed from December 2006 through March 2007, and revealed that in all cases, patients required surgical intervention to correct or remove the device.

CONCLUSIONS

The medical device recall process is complex, requiring the coordination and timely action of potentially thousands of parties. It is an important tool used by firms and FDA to protect the public and mitigate health risks from unsafe or ineffective devices. While the recall process may not eliminate 100 percent of health risks associated with recalled devices, careful implementation and evaluation are critical to minimizing health risks.

FDA has a key role in identifying and minimizing the public health risks presented by defective or unsafe devices. In this regard, FDA has opportunities to close some of the gaps that currently exist in the medical device recall process, and enhance its oversight of device recalls. As currently structured, FDA's approach to oversight of medical device recalls is reactive—responding to individual recalls as they occur. Rather than pursuing a strictly case-by-case approach to overseeing recalls, FDA could take a more proactive approach to its oversight. The agency has a plethora of data available on thousands of recalls, but at present, is not effectively reviewing and analyzing these data in a systematic manner. More routine analyses of these data could help FDA identify trends in the numbers and types of devices being recalled, as well as the underlying causes of device recalls. Such information would provide FDA with a better understanding of the risks presented by defective or unsafe devices, which could lead the agency to proactively identify strategies and measures needed to address systemic problems with the design or manufacture of individual devices or entire categories of devices. Armed with the results of these types of analyses, FDA could then be in a position to help mitigate safety risks before they occur, and thus minimize the need for recalls. This is particularly important for the devices involved in the highest-risk recalls, which place the public at risk of serious health consequences, including death.

Furthermore, while the agency has devoted substantial resources to monitoring individual recalls, opportunities for enhancing its oversight of specific recalls also exist. A key FDA mechanism for overseeing individual recalls—audit checks of a small portion of customers and device users involved in the recall—are often implemented inconsistently. This is due to unclear procedures that investigators are using for implementing and documenting audit checks and making their final assessments. As a result, investigators can make inconsistent determinations about whether firms, customers, and device users have effectively conducted a recall. Additionally, FDA lacks clear criteria for determining whether firms have successfully completed recalls, and has failed to maintain important documentation justifying its decisions to terminate the highest-risk recalls. This impedes independent assessments of FDA's decision making and leaves the agency vulnerable to questions about the basis it used to determine that recalling firms fulfilled all their responsibilities when conducting recalls. By addressing these weaknesses, FDA could reduce the risk that defective or unsafe medical devices remain on the market, potentially endangering public health.

RECOMMENDATIONS FOR EXECUTIVE ACTION

To enhance FDA's oversight of medical device recalls, and in particular, those medical device recalls that pose the highest risk, we recommend that the Commissioner of FDA take the following four actions:

- Create a program to routinely and systematically assess medical device recall information, and use this information to proactively identify strategies for mitigating health risks presented by defective or unsafe devices. This assessment should be designed, at a minimum, to identify trends in the numbers and types of recalls, devices most frequently being recalled, and underlying causes of recalls.
- Clarify procedures for conducting medical device recall audit checks to improve the ability of investigators to perform these checks in a consistent manner.
- Develop explicit criteria for assessing whether recalling firms have performed an effective correction or removal action.
- Document the agency's basis for terminating individual recalls.

AGENCY COMMENTS

We provided a draft of this report to HHS for review. HHS's written comments are reprinted in appendix III. HHS agreed with our conclusions and recommendations and stated that the agency is committed to exploring each of our recommendations fully. HHS reported that FDA plans to convene a working group to both evaluate improvements to the recall process and to develop strategies to implement our recommendations. According to HHS, FDA recognizes that standardized guidance will strengthen the management of the recall process. In addition, HHS elaborated on some of FDA's efforts to enhance its oversight by, for example, developing more routine analysis and reporting of recall data. HHS also provided technical comments, which we incorporated as appropriate. We are greatly encouraged by the agency's response, and believe its expeditious implementation of the recommendations will serve to enhance the safety of medical devices used by millions of Americans each day.

As agreed with your offices, unless you publicly announce the contents of this report earlier, we plan no further distribution until 30 days from the report date. At that time, we will send copies to the Commissioner of FDA and appropriate congressional committees. The report also will be available at no charge on GAO's Web site at http://www.gao.gov.

If you or your staffs have any questions about this report, please contact me at (202) 512-7114 or crossem@gao.gov. Contact points for our Offices of Congressional Relations and Public Affairs may be found on the last page of this report. GAO staff who made major contributions to this report are listed in appendix IV.

Marcia Crosse
Director, Health Care

APPENDIX I. TOOLS TO HELP IDENTIFY RECALLED DEVICES AND PLANNED INITIATIVES FOR ASSISTING WITH DEVICE RECALLS

Several key stakeholders involved in the medical device recall process, including recalling firms, device distributors, and device users—such as hospitals—share responsibilities for effectively implementing recalls. To implement an effective recall, stakeholders need mechanisms to ensure timely and open communication about the recalls, and a means of locating devices subject to recall. This appendix describes the recall notification and tracking systems available to help manage device recalls. It also provides information on the status of the Food and Drug Administration's (FDA) unique device identification (UDI) initiative—which is intended to enable the identification of a device throughout distribution and use.

To obtain this information, we interviewed officials from FDA and key stakeholders, including representatives of firms providing subscription-based recall alert information, manufacturers, distributors, group purchasing organizations, hospital systems, and patient safety groups. Through these interviews we obtained information on what these stakeholders considered to be the key challenges they face in implementing device recalls. We also obtained information about mechanisms which, in particular, hospital systems use to help identify devices subject to recall. Further, we reviewed FDA's progress in implementing its UDI initiative. To accomplish this, we examined published studies on this initiative, reviewed stakeholder comments submitted for FDA's public meetings on the UDI, and interviewed FDA officials responsible for managing the UDI program.[41]

Many Stakeholders Use Electronic Recall Notification and Tracking Systems to Help Manage Device Recalls

We learned through stakeholder interviews that instead of relying solely on notifications from medical device manufacturers, health care providers and other stakeholders have come to rely on other sources of information to stay abreast of potential recalls. Furthermore, these electronic communication technologies are evolving and, over time, stakeholders have begun recognizing that they can play a role in helping to effectively implement recalls.

Our interviews with stakeholders revealed that a number of different privately developed, subscription-based electronic notification and tracking systems are available to help identify and process recalls. Stakeholders indicated that these systems are primarily used by hospitals, but that the systems are available to others involved in recalls as well. Available services identify recalls from a number of sources, including device manufacturers and FDA's Web site. The services compile lists of recalls and send electronic messages about recalls to paid subscribers. These services vary in sophistication and price. One service we learned about was limited to periodic electronic notification of all recalls at a cost of about $500 per year. Others include software to help individual hospitals specifically delegate responsibility within their hospital system to specific officials who will manage certain aspects of the recalls—such as removing recalled products from inventory—and for tracking the progress of the recalls. These systems can cost several thousand dollars per year. Owners of these systems that we spoke to indicated that hundreds of hospitals subscribe to their systems (see table 5).

Stakeholders we interviewed identified several operational benefits of using recall notification systems. First, they indicated these systems allow for an increased ability to identify the universe of recalls rather than simply relying on receiving notices from recalling firms. Second, stakeholders indicated that quality assurance measures used by the systems help ensure that the recall notifications contain sufficiently detailed and accurate information. They indicated that personnel working for such systems will review the recall notifications they compile prior to sending them to the subscribers. If needed, those providing the recall alert services will contact the recalling firm and update the notice for the subscribers if information is unclear or missing.

Table 5. Examples of Available Recall Alert Services

Type of system	Service provided	Primary customers	Source of information in alerts
E-mail alerts	Sends e-mail alerts to hospitals every 7-10 days or immediately for urgent recalls.	Hospitals	FDA, manufacturers, and subscribers
Weekly newsletter, Web-based alerts and tracking	An alert service and optional Web-based recall and safety alert tracking system that helps clients to acquire, distribute, and manage recalls.	Primarily hospitals, but also government agencies and manufacturers	FDA, manufacturers, and subscribers
Web-based customized alerts and tracking	A customized Web-based recall management service that alerts appropriate personnel of recalls and allows them to track a recall's progress.	Designed for hospitals but used by others including outpatient centers, nursing homes, and day care centers	FDA, manufacturers, subscribers, U.S. Army Medical Material Agency, and Consumer Products Safety Commission

Source: GAO analysis of information from medical device recall stakeholders.

Third, stakeholders indicated that such systems can help ensure that recall notifications are routed to specific personnel within an institution responsible for managing the recall, reducing the likelihood that implementing the recall is delayed or overlooked. Officials from some hospitals we spoke with indicated that manufacturers will frequently notify the department in a hospital that received the product, which may not be the best point of contact for ensuring recalled devices are corrected or removed. However, one hospital system indicated that by using the more sophisticated alert systems, they are able to automatically forward recall alerts to key personnel specifically identified by the hospital. This ensures that only the appropriate departments at the hospital are alerted. Finally, stakeholders stated that these systems allow hospitals to identify and process recalls sooner.

Status of UDI Initiative

The Food and Drug Administration Amendments Act of 2007 (FDAAA) required FDA to develop a UDI system—a major initiative to better track and identify devices.[42] Through the UDI, FDA plans to require that the label of a device bear a unique identifier that is able to identify the device throughout its distribution and use. Figure 8 displays an example of the key attributes that might be included in a UDI. In this example, the label includes key information, such as a device's lot number and expiration date which could be scanned into databases.

FDA has been working on the UDI since 2005, prior to the enactment of FDAAA, and has made some preliminary decisions about the system. According to FDA, it currently has a proposed schedule that calls for implementation of the UDI in phases over several years.

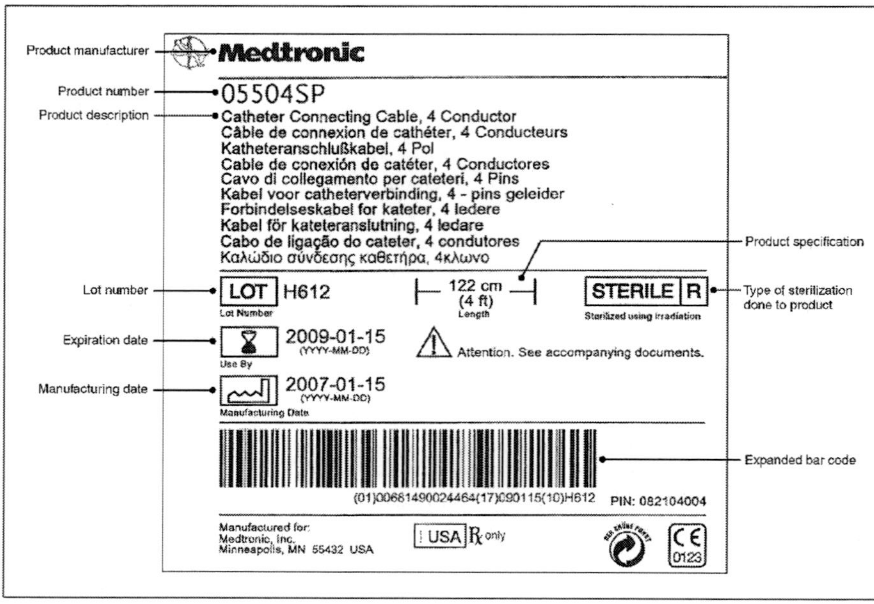

Source: Medtronic.

Figure 8. Example of a Potential Unique Device Identification Label.

Key activities completed for the UDI include the following.

- April 14-15, 2005: FDA held a workshop to obtain comments from various stakeholders on the UDI. A draft report about the UDI prepared by a contractor for FDA, known as "The White Paper," was provided to attendees prior to the workshop to use as background for workshop discussions.

- August 17, 2005: The White Paper was issued and provided information on technologies and standards available for the UDI initiative and the possible benefits of automatic identification of devices. The paper also identified key issues FDA should consider moving forward, including costs of the UDI. Also, the paper incorporated stakeholder comments from the workshop held in April 2005.[43]
- March 22, 2006: Another contractor issued a report outlining the possible benefits of the UDI and decisions FDA must make to implement the system, including the technology needed to use the UDI.[44]
- August 11, 2006: FDA formally solicited comments in the Federal Register for the UDI initiative.[45]
- September 27, 2007: FDAAA enacted, requiring FDA to develop and implement the UDI.
- February 12, 2009: FDA held a public workshop on the UDI to identify remaining issues related to the establishment of a UDI system and to request comments on this topic.
- November 20, 2009: FDA published the results of a pilot test of the UDI. The results included several recommendations for the future of the UDI including specific enhancements that could enhance the UDI's functionality.[46]
- November 30, 2010: Another report on pilot activities was published containing feedback from organizations that will label the devices and internal FDA stakeholders. The report stated that fewer concerns remain as FDA is close to releasing the UDI regulation.[47]

According to FDA, the UDI implementation schedule calls for a phased approach that will take several years to reach full-scale implementation. FDA is currently working on a proposed rule and intends to publish it and seek public comments in spring 2011, and issue a final rule 12 to 18 months later. According to FDA's senior advisor for the UDI, the proposed rule will include several key decisions that FDA, based on its prior studies, has reached regarding the UDI. These key decisions include the following.

- Provisions for a UDI database that FDA will maintain. Manufacturers will send key information about their devices to FDA, which will maintain a database containing a device identifier for all devices distributed in the United States.

- Flexibility to allow manufacturers to decide how to label their devices using automatic identification and data capture. This could mean using a linear or two-dimensional bar code, or radio frequency identification.[48]

  In addition, FDA indicated that there are other issues for which they have not yet made final decisions, and they are still assessing these before they issue a proposed rule. These include the following.
- The labeling requirements for different devices, for example, riskier devices may be labeled with a unique identifier individually, while disposable, low-risk devices may be labeled based on how they are packaged (e.g., bandages will have their UDI identifier on their box).
- If the UDI should have a phased implementation schedule for administering the identifiers, for example, class III devices—the most risky devices, including some that are implantable—may use the UDI within 1 year of publishing the final rule, while class II and class I devices might follow meeting the UDI requirement within 3 and 5 years, respectively.

Figure 9 presents a timeline of key activities since FDA began assessing the UDI and its planned implementation schedule.

An FDA official said that the agency expects that the UDI will provide benefits beyond increased precision in identifying recalled devices, and that some benefits of the UDI will be realized immediately after its implementation. According to the UDI senior advisor, these benefits include improved tracking of adverse events associated with medical devices and prevention of device counterfeiting. He also stated that many manufacturers already use identifiers on their devices and should have little problem adapting to the new UDI system.

Despite the potential benefits of the UDI, some stakeholders expressed concern that the success of UDIs depends on hospitals' ability to utilize these identifiers, and that it may be years before the benefits to the recall process are realized. Manufacturers we contacted stated that many hospitals do not use the lot and serial numbers currently provided by manufacturers to track devices, and FDA does not have authority to require providers to use the UDI. This concern was also reflected in comments from officials at several hospitals that we contacted. Some indicated that they do not have inventory systems in place that enable them to track devices throughout their hospitals. Therefore, they must manually search their inventory, sometimes at multiple locations.

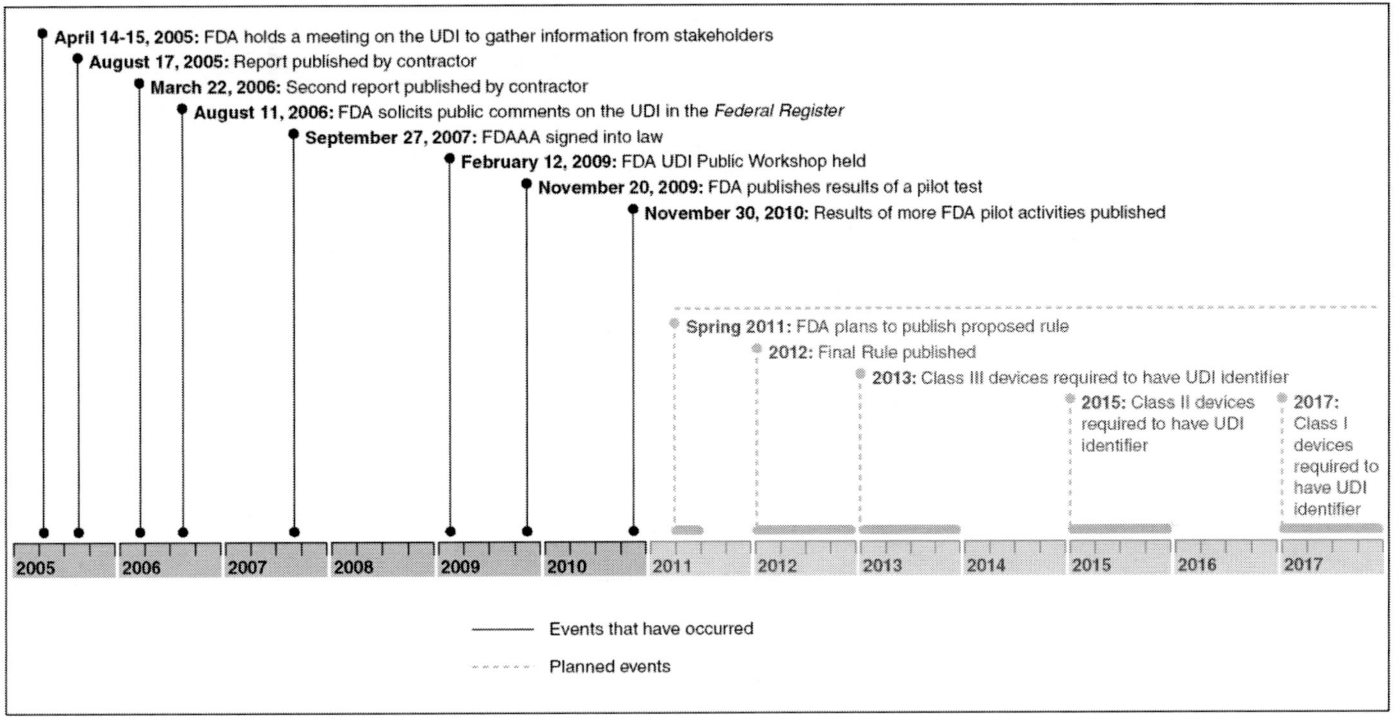

Source: GAO analysis of FDA information.

Figure 9. Timeline of Events for the Development of the Unique Device Identification Initiative.

Locating a recalled device can be particularly difficult because a device may contain multiple identification numbers assigned by manufacturers and distributors for their own tracking purposes. Without upgrades to these hospitals' systems, officials acknowledged that the UDI will be less effective in enhancing patient safety. FDA's UDI senior advisor stated that larger hospitals might be more eager to adopt the technology necessary to track devices using the UDI once it is implemented, but acknowledged that benefits for the recall process are greatly dependent on hospitals' implementation of the UDI, which could take up to 10 years for many hospitals, especially smaller ones.

Appendix II. Class I Medical Device Recalls from Our Sample for Which Firms Were Unable to Correct or Remove All Devices

In some instances recalling firms are not able to correct or remove all of the devices subject to a recall. Of the 53 class I recalls in our sample of recalls that were initiated during the period of January 1, 2005, through December 31, 2009, there were recalled medical devices that firms were unable to correct or remove. Table 6 includes information on the number of devices subject to these 21 recalls, the number corrected or removed, and if available, reasons firms provided to FDA explaining why they could not correct or remove 100 percent of the devices.

Table 6. Class I Medical Device Recalls for Which Firms Were Unable to Correct or Remove All Devices

Recalled device	Reason for recall	Number of Devices recalled[a]	Number of devices corrected orremoved[a]	Number of devices outstanding[a]	Reasons for incomplete recovery
Centrifuge rotor	Catastrophic failure or explosion	42[b]	32[b]	10[b]	Could not locate some users or devices
Endoscopic injector	Could inject into vital organ and cause death	9,984	4,114	5,870	Users could not locate many devices, others were already used

Recalled device	Reason for recall	Number of Devices recalled[a]	Number of devices corrected orremoved[a]	Number of devices outstanding[a]	Reasons for incomplete recovery
Insulin syringe	Package mislabeled, contains incorrect dose of insulin	471,000	61,351	409,649	Probably used by consumers or thrown away
Intra-aortic balloon and control system	Fault in connector may result in incorrect pump volume	13,570[b]	1,174[b]	12,396[b]	Some users did not respond, other devices were already used
Blood glucose test strip	Counterfeit device results in inaccurate test results	5,292	1,786	3,506	Presumed used or thrown away
Denervation probe	Mislabeled as sterile	539[c]	27[c]	512[c]	Many users sterilized devices them-selves and then used them
Heating pad	Electrical problems, leading to fires, burns, and property damage	408,599	119	408,480	Firm assumed most had been disposed of (recall was initiated 6 years after m-anufacturing)
Glucose monitoring system	Displaying American units for Canadian customers	33[b]	32[b]	1[b]	Recalling firm could not locate the device
Infusion set	Improper venting, leading to fluctuating insulin delivery	Unknown[d]	424,506	Unknown[d]	Single-use sets; impossible to know how many were available for use
Ventricular catheter	Catheter becomes detached from base after implantation	3,048	Unknown[d]	Unknown[d]	Recalling firm did not indicate final disposition of all recalled devices

Table 6. (Continued)

Recalled device	Reason for recall	Number of Devices recalled[a]	Number of devices corrected orremoved[a]	Number of devices outstanding[a]	Reasons for incomplete recovery
IV extension sets	Manufacturing defect, possibly resulting in improper functioning and embolism	99	56	43	No reason given
Needle and infusion sets	Needles "punch out," sending the core into a patient's body	Unknown[d]	13,988	Unknown[d]	Firm did not list total number of devices or all devices were recovered
Ventilator	Flow valve failures	277	276	1	Missing from a nursing home (police report was filed)
Ventilator	Power supply failures	2,270	Unknown[d]	Unknown[d]	Recalling firm could not account for all devices and noted that some customers did not respond
Catheter	Catheter may crack	70	55	15	Devices were used
Automatic implantable cardioverter defibrillator	Possible short-circuiting of the device	14,010	13,839	171	Sold, but no implant record available
Pacemaker	Device's seal may degrade allowing excess moisture within the pacemaker	23,987	22,255	1,732	Sold, but no implant record available
Implantable programmable pump	Pumps may detach, interrupting drug flow	1,742	1,497	245	Some devices remain implanted or have an undetermined status

Recalled device	Reason for recall	Number of Devices recalled[a]	Number of devices corrected orremoved[a]	Number of devices outstanding[a]	Reasons for incomplete recovery
Implantable program-able pump	Pump motor may stall causing drug delivery to stop abruptly	23,895[c]	Unknown[d]	Unknown[d]	Hundreds of users did not reply
Carotid stent system	Possible detachment in the stent delivery system	1,570	619	951	Devices were either used or disposed at the users' facilities
Implantable defibrillator	Potential for a short circuit and loss of	6,911	6,787	124	Sold, but no implant record available

Source: GAO analysis of FDA recall files.

[a]Numbers reflect units of distribution. In some cases, devices are sold individually, and in other instances multiple devices are sold in a package (e.g., glucose strips).

[b]Includes units distributed to Canada.

[c]Includes worldwide units.

[d]Documentation provided by FDA did not include these numbers.

APPENDIX III. COMMENTS FROM THE DEPARTMENT OF HEALTH AND HUMAN SERVICES

DEPARTMENT OF HEALTH & HUMAN SERVICES

Office of the Assistant Secretary for Legislation

Washington, D.C. 20201

MAY 26 2011

Marcia Crosse
Director, Health Care
U.S. Government Accountability Office
441 G Street N.W.
Washington, DC 20548

Dear Ms. Crosse:

Attached are comments on the U.S. Government Accountability Office's (GAO) draft report entitled, "MEDICAL DEVICES: FDA Should Enhance Its Oversight of Recalls" (GAO-11-468).

The Department appreciates the opportunity to review this draft report prior to publication.

Sincerely,

Jim R. Esquea
Assistant Secretary for Legislation

Attachment

GENERAL COMMENTS OF THE DEPARTMENT OF HEALTH AND HUMAN SERVICES (HHS) ON THE GOVERNMENT ACCOUNTABILITY OFFICE'S (GAO) DRAFT REPORT ENTITLED, "MEDICAL DEVICES: FDA SHOULD ENHANCE ITS OVERSIGHT OF RECALLS" (GAO-11-468)

The Department appreciates the opportunity to review and comment on this draft report.

In general, the Food and Drug Administration (FDA) believes GAO's draft report accurately describes the FDA's medical device recall program. The agency agrees with GAO's conclusions and recommendations and is committed to exploring each recommendation fully and to making appropriate implementation decisions based on the results of its internal analysis.

The FDA agrees that agency recall data is a robust resource, the assessment of which can help mitigate health risks presented by defective or unsafe devices. The FDA also agrees that the agency does not currently conduct some of the analyses described in the GAO report. Although industry is responsible for analysis of design and manufacturing-related risks of individual medical devices, the FDA has an important role in recall data analysis and performs a variety of routine analyses to inform its regulatory activities. The FDA compiles recall information for every product code (medical device type), each medical device brand name, and every individual firm. The FDA aggregates recall information on related products for each 510(k) submission reviewed, each Establishment Inspection Report (EIR) review, and all adverse event analyses. The FDA's risk-based work plan uses recall data as one data source to identify types of medical devices and industry segments that should be priorities for inspection. Likewise, the FDA uses recall data to support its risk-based site selection model, which identifies individual facilities likely to have quality system violations. Every cross-Center team begins with a recall analysis similar to that provided for the Automated External Defibrillator effort cited in the GAO report. Recent cross-Center teams have focused on infusion pumps and ventilators.

Recommendation 1: Create a program to routinely and systematically assess medical device recall information, and use this information to proactively identify strategies for mitigating health risks presented by defective or unsafe devices. This assessment should be designed, at a minimum, to identify trends in the numbers and types of recalls, devices most frequently being recalled, and underlying causes of recalls.

The FDA agrees it should assess medical device recall information more routinely and systematically, and that it should use this information to mitigate health risks. The FDA plans to perform a systematic evaluation of potential recall analyses. The agency plans to consider recall processing times, recalled device types and medical specialties, types of device failures observed, quality of recall notifications, and other elements that elevate the risk to public health. Based on the evaluation, the agency will develop more routine analysis and reporting. In the meantime, the FDA plans to continue to analyze numbers and types of recalls on a yearly basis.

Recommendation 2: Clarify procedures for conducting medical device recall audit checks to improve the ability of investigators to perform these checks in a consistent manner.

GENERAL COMMENTS OF THE DEPARTMENT OF HEALTH AND HUMAN SERVICES (HHS) ON THE GOVERNMENT ACCOUNTABILITY OFFICE'S (GAO) DRAFT REPORT ENTITLED, "MEDICAL DEVICES: FDA SHOULD ENHANCE ITS OVERSIGHT OF RECALLS" (GAO-11-468)

The FDA generally agrees it should update and clarify its recall audit check procedures and is committed to reevaluating its procedures for conducting recall audit checks. In recent years, the agency has experienced significant increases in the number of recalls of FDA-regulated products, some of which involve the largest and most complex recalls in FDA history. To address these issues and to better understand the current recall business processes, the FDA has undertaken a recall process improvement study that is intended to examine the overall recall process in protecting the public health and removing violative products from the marketplace. This study was recently completed, and the FDA plans to convene a working group to evaluate the results and to develop a strategy for the implementation of the recommendations. Furthermore, the FDA will continually review its recall procedures to determine whether specific additions, updates, and clarifications may be needed to the recall program, including the audit check process.

In addition, the FDA has already begun implementing some initiatives for improving the recall audit check process, which currently is manual, for all FDA-regulated products. For example, and as noted in GAO's report, the FDA has invested in automating its current recall audit check process, which will allow the agency to automate the creation, issuance, assigning, and tracking of recall audit check assignments, as well as to establish an electronic mechanism for reporting or documenting recall audit check results.

Recommendation 3: Develop explicit criteria for assessing whether recalling firms have performed an effective correction or removal action.

The FDA generally agrees it should clarify its criteria for assessing whether recalling firms have performed an effective correction or removal action. The FDA acknowledges it needs to update its process and procedures, and recognizes that standardized guidance will strengthen the management of the recall process and promote a consistent approach for assessing recalling firms' efforts and effectiveness in correcting or removing violative products from the marketplace. The FDA is committed to continually analyzing the procedures and the criteria it uses to determine when recalling firms have performed an effective correction or removal action. The FDA working group which will be tasked with evaluating the results of the recently completed recall process improvement study will use the study results to develop an informed strategy for implementing this recommendation.

Recommendation 4: Document the agency's basis for terminating individual recalls.

The FDA generally agrees that the agency should document its termination decisions and is committed to reevaluating its recall termination procedures and documentation. The FDA working group that will be tasked with evaluating the results of the recently-completed recall process improvement study will consider the study results to make recommendations to FDA management on the need for specific additions, updates, and clarifications to the recall termination process.

Appendix IV. GAO Contact and Staff Acknowledgments

Staff Acknowledgments

In addition to the contact named above, Geri Redican-Bigott, Assistant Director; Kaycee Glavich; Cathleen Hamann; Eagan Kemp; Julian Klazkin; Zachary Levinson; David Lichtenfeld; Daniel Ries; Christina C. Serna; and Katherine Wunderink made key contributions to this report.

End Notes

[1] 21 U.S.C. § 360h(e), 21 C.F.R. pt. 810 (2010). The steps that FDA follows for such mandatory recalls are separate and distinct from those followed during a voluntary recall. The steps that FDA follows during voluntary recalls are described at subpart C, part 7, of title 21 of the Code of Federal Regulations.

[2] For purposes of this report, we use the term guidance to refer to FDA's advice or recommendations to recalling firms managing voluntary recalls and the term procedures to refer to FDA's instructions to agency staff overseeing these recalls.

[3] GAO, *Medical Devices: FDA Can Improve Oversight of Tracking and Recall Systems*, GAO/HEHS-98-211 (Washington, D.C.: Sept. 24, 1998).

[4] GAO, *Medical Devices: FDA's Premarket Review and Postmarket Safety Efforts*, GAO-11-556T (Washington, D.C.: Apr. 13, 2011).

[5] While FDA has authority to order a mandatory recall, it did not exercise this authority during the period we reviewed. See 21 U.S.C. § 360h(e), 21 C.F.R. pt. 810 (2010). Also, our information does not include devices that a firm may have voluntarily taken off the market for other, less serious, reasons. For example, a market withdrawal is a firm's correction or removal of a distributed device that involves no violation or a minor violation of the laws FDA administers and for which FDA would not initiate legal action. 21 C.F.R. § 806.2(h) (2010). A stock recovery is a firm's correction or removal of a device that has not been marketed or that has not left the direct control of the manufacturer. 21 C.F.R § 806.2(l) (2010). FDA does not consider market withdrawals and stock recoveries to be recalls.

[6] FDA tracks recalls by both the recall event, that is, the actual process of implementing a recall, and the products being recalled. A single recall event could involve multiple products (e.g., different sizes and models of the same device). We use the term recall in the report to refer to recall events.

[7] The status of the recalls is as of April 16, 2010, the date FDA provided us with the extract from RES.

[8] See GAO, *Standards for Internal Control in the Federal Government*, GAO/AIMD-00-21.3.1 (Washington, D.C.: Nov. 1999).

[9] A small percentage of devices enter the market by other means, such as through the humanitarian device exemption process that allows market entry, without adherence to certain requirements, for devices benefiting patients with rare diseases or conditions. See 21 U.S.C. § 360j(m), 21 C.F.R. pt. 814, subpart H (2010). In addition, many other less risky types of class I and II devices are also exempt from FDA's premarket review.

[10] *Substantial equivalence or substantially equivalent* means that the device has the same intended use as another legally marketed device and the same technological characteristics, or that the device has different technological characteristics and information submitted to FDA demonstrates that the device is as safe and effective as the legally marketed device and does not raise different questions of safety or effectiveness. 21 U.S.C. § 360c(i)(1)(A).

[11] According to FDA, performance testing results should be submitted if there are important descriptive differences between the device and other devices of the same type or if the descriptive characteristics for the new device are not precise enough to ensure comparability. In these instances, the most appropriate bench testing, animal testing, or both to address the performance issue should be provided, and summary information on the testing should generally suffice.

[12] From 2003 through 2007, 79 percent of the riskiest medical devices (class III devices) were approved through the PMA process. As we reported in 2009, FDA has cleared some class III devices through the 510(k) process, rather than approving the devices through the more stringent PMA process. See GAO, *Medical Devices: FDA Should Take Steps to Ensure That High-Risk Device Types Are Approved Through the Most Stringent Premarket Review Process*, GAO-09-190 (Washington, D.C.: Jan. 15, 2009).

[13] 21 C.F.R. § 7.3(g) (2010). A removal is the physical removal of a device from its point of use to some other location for repair, modification, adjustment, relabeling, destruction, or inspection. A correction may involve these actions without the physical removal of a device from its point of use. 21 C.F.R. § 806.2(d, i) (2010).

[14] Stakeholders such as distributors and device users, and anyone else who received, purchased, or used the product being recalled are referred to as "consignees." 21 C.F.R. §§ 7.3(n), 806.2(c) (2010). In this report, we generally refer to these entities as customers and device users.

[15] A given recall may involve a single device or multiple devices. For example, a recall may include different sizes of the same device, or a device made up of multiple components (i.e., screws, bolts, tubes).

[16] The firm will contact one of FDA's district offices depending upon the location from which it chooses to manage the recall. This district will have primary responsibility for monitoring the recall. Each district has a recall coordinator, who among other duties, processes medical device recalls and monitors the progress of the firm's actions.

[17] 21 C.F.R. § 806.10(a), (b) (2010). Reports are not required for recalls involving problematic devices that do not pose a health risk.

[18] FDA officials indicated that although this time frame was in effect at the time of our review, they have recently adjusted classification time frames, which now range from 26 to 40 days depending on the nature of the recall.

[19] See 21 C.F.R. § 7.3(m) (2010).

[20] Audit checks, which generally cover from 2 to 10 percent of the total number of distributors and device users, are typically conducted by FDA on class I and class II recalls. Audit checks are generally not conducted on class III recalls. Audit checks are separate from effectiveness checks, which are conducted by the recalling firm.

[21] A firm's completion of a recall does not necessarily indicate that it corrected or removed 100 percent of the recalled devices, but rather that it made reasonable efforts to contact those affected by the recall and obtained as many devices as possible.

[22] General hospital and personal use devices include bandages, examination gowns, infusion pumps, and stretchers. Diagnostic chemistry devices include test systems, such as those for blood glucose.

[23] Information on mode of market entry—PMA, 510(k), or exempt—was missing for 737 (21 percent) of the 3,510 recalls. Our analysis is therefore based on the available data related to 2,773 recalls.

[24] This includes recalls involving multiple devices (such as kits containing a pump and a catheter) some of which were cleared through the 510(k) process, and others approved through the

PMA process. It also includes devices that are exempt from FDA review, such as most class I devices.

[25] Information on mode of market entry—PMA, 510(k), or exempt—was missing for 30 (23 percent) of the 131 class I recalls that occurred during calendar years 2005 through 2009. Therefore, our above analysis is based on the available data related to 101 recalls.

[26] Two separate studies also analyzed class I recalls from 2005 to 2009 and found similar statistics as ours. See D. Zukerman, Paul Brown, Steven Nissen, *Medical Device Recalls and the FDA Approval Process. Archives of Internal Medicine* (Feb. 14, 2011) and related testimony at U.S. House of Representatives, Energy and Commerce Subcommittee on Health Hearing on "Impact of Medical Device Regulation on Jobs and Patients" (Feb. 17, 2011). See also R. Hall, *Using Recall Data to Assess the 510(k) Process. Presentation at Institutes of Medicine Meeting* (July 28, 2010) and related testimony at U.S. House of Representatives, Energy and Commerce Subcommittee on Health, Hearing on "Impact of Medical Device Regulation on Jobs and Patients" (Feb. 17, 2011).

[27] Of the 2,050 medical device recalls that had been terminated, 22 were missing valid termination dates and hence were not included in our analysis.

[28] According to FDA, in some cases a firm initiates a recall without contacting FDA, thus the agency may not learn about the recall until a much later date.

[29] We previously reported that FDA failed to meet its 90-day termination guideline in 33 percent of the 36 recalls we reviewed. See GAO/HEHS-98-211.

[30] We previously reported on the importance of establishing and using metrics as a management tool. See, for example, GAO, *Food and Drug Administration: Opportunities Exist to Better Address Management Challenges*, GAO-10-279 (Washington, D.C.: Feb. 19, 2010).

[31] We previously reported that FDA faced challenges fulfilling and managing its growing medical product oversight responsibilities and should develop complete estimates of its resource needs. See GAO, *Food and Drug Administration: FDA Faces Challenges Meeting Its Growing Medical Product Responsibilities and Should Develop Complete Estimates of Its Resource Needs*, GAO-09-581 (Washington, D.C.: June 19, 2009).

[32] Statement of Dr. William Maisel, CDRH Deputy Director for Science, at FDA Public Workshop on External Defibrillators (Washington, D.C.: Dec. 15-16, 2010).

[33] According to FDA, this initiative also includes plans to develop strategies for improving CDRH's processes for classifying recalls and notifying the public about recalls.

[34] For 4 of the 53 recalls we reviewed, FDA identified the problem that led to the recalls through postmarket establishment inspections, unrelated to recalls. Thus, FDA did not need to conduct initial recall inspections.

[35] FDA's guidance at the time of our review recommended that CDRH classify a recall within 31 calendar days of obtaining information needed to classify the recall.

[36] We obtained the current status of these recalls through our reviews of the recall files and discussions with FDA district office officials. These discussions took place between December 2010 and February 2011.

[37] FDA's procedures note that audit checks should be conducted for all class I recalls. In 8 of the 53 recalls FDA did not conduct audit checks. In six of these cases, the recall file contained written documentation explaining why audit checks were not conducted.

[38] For 2 of the 45 recalls there was evidence that FDA conducted audit checks, but FDA did not provide copies of the audit check forms. Thus, the 2,196 audit checks forms we reviewed were for a total of 43 recalls.

[39] For two recalls, FDA was unable to locate the audit check forms. Thus, we have excluded these recalls from the calculation of the average number of audit checks.

[40] See GAO/AIMD-00-21.3.1.

[41] Published studies we reviewed include: Eastern Research Group, Inc., *ERG Final Report: Unique Identification for Medical Devices*, a report prepared for FDA, March 2006, and Susan J. Griffey, Andy Martin, Marjorie Odle, and M.J. Wylie, *SSS-GHX Development of*

the Prototype Unique Device Identifier Database: Report of a Pilot Test on Usability and Feasibility, a report prepared for FDA, (November 2009).

[42] Pub. L. No. 110-85, § 226, 121 Stat. 823, 854.

[43] The ECRI Institute, *Task 4 White Paper - Automatic Identification of Medical Devices - Final Version*, a report prepared for FDA, August 2005.

[44] Eastern Research Group, Inc., *ERG Final Report: Unique Identification for Medical Devices*, a report prepared for FDA, March 2006.

[45] Docket No. FDA-2008-N-0661, CDRH 200866. Unique Device Identification System; Public Workshop; Request for Comments.

[46] Susan J. Griffey, Andy Martin, Marjorie Odle, MJ Wylie, *SSS-GHX Development of the Prototype Unique Device Identifier Database: Report of a Pilot Test on Usability and Feasibility*, a report prepared for FDA, (November 2009).

[47] FDA, *Results of FDA Pilot Activities To Explore Opportunities and Challenges With the Implementation of a Unique Device Identifier System* (Washington, D.C., 2010).

[48] A two-dimensional barcode stores information horizontally and vertically allowing the two-dimensional barcodes to store more information than linear bar codes, which store information only horizontally. Radio frequency identification allows for information about a device to be transmitted between a tag on the device and a reader using radio waves.

CHAPTER SOURCES

Chapter 1 - This is an edited, reformatted and augmented version of a U.S. Government Accountibility Office publication, GAO-11-603, dated June 2011.

Chapter 2 - This is an edited, reformatted and augmented version of a U.S. Government Accountibility Office publication, GAO-11-468, dated June 2011.

INDEX

A

B

C

D

E

F

S

T

U

V

W